What people are saying about

A Little Bigfoot: On the Hunt in Sumatra

Pat Spain is that rare thing: a rationalist who still embraces the possible and knows that there are more things in heaven and earth than are dreamt of. A grown-up who has lost none of the childhood wonder and curiosity that makes the world magical. A scientist who keeps an open mind and rejoices in the fact that absence of proof is not proof of absence. There is nobody I'd want to travel with more to explore the wild side of our literally extraordinary planet. Buckle up and prepare for adventures.
Harry Marshall, Chairman and Co-Founder of Icon Films

If you loved *Beast Hunter* about the legends of mythical creatures, you're going to love this book even more. It's the "making of" told as only someone like Pat can. A true page turner!
Haley Chamberlain Nelson, science journalist

If I was lost in a Victorian-styled deep virgin jungle, surrounded by a variety of poisonous plants, venomous reptiles, and stinging flying insects, there's no one I'd rather have by my side to help navigate me to safety than explorer Patrick Spain. Short of having Pat with all of us field workers for every trek, thank goodness we now have this remarkable insightful volume to open our eyes further.
Loren Coleman, Director of the International Cryptozoology Museum and author of *The Field Guide to Bigfoot and Other Mystery Primates*

Titles in the On the Hunt series

A Little Bigfoot: On the Hunt in Sumatra

or, How I Learned There Are Some Things That Really Do Not Taste Like Chicken

A Little Bigfoot:
On the Hunt
in Sumatra

or, How I Learned There Are Some
Things That Really Do Not Taste
Like Chicken

Pat Spain

6TH
BOOKS

Winchester, UK
Washington, USA

JOHN HUNT PUBLISHING

First published by Sixth Books, 2022
Sixth Books is an imprint of John Hunt Publishing Ltd., No. 3 East St., Alresford,
Hampshire SO24 9EE, UK
office@jhpbooks.com
www.johnhuntpublishing.com
www.6th-books.com

For distributor details and how to order please visit the 'Ordering' section on our website.

ISBN: 978 1 78904 605 2
978 1 78904 606 9 (ebook)
Library of Congress Control Number: 2020942271

A CIP catalogue record for this book is available from the British Library.

Design: Stuart Davies

UK: Printed and bound by CPI Group (UK) Ltd, Croydon, CR0 4YY
Printed in North America by CPI GPS partners

We operate a distinctive and ethical publishing philosophy in
all areas of our business, from our global network of authors to
production and worldwide distribution.

Contents

This book is for my grandmother, Nana Felecia. Nana read more than anyone I've ever met. Her apartment was stacked with books – floor to ceiling in most rooms, lining every wall. I loved it in there – the feel of those books. When she read what I'd written and told me it was "really good" it meant something special to me, and made me think I might actually be able to create something that other people would want to read.

Introduction

Some of you may know me as the "(almost) King of the Jungle", "Legend Hunter", "that animal guy", "Beast Hunter" or "that guy who had cancer and catches snakes". Probably not, though. Despite having a couple dozen hours of international TV series to my name, and giving hundreds of talks and presentations, I don't really get recognized very often – unless we're talking about college kids in Guwahati, India, middle-aged men in the US, or preteen Indonesian girls. My key demographics, it turns out. I struggle to name anything those groups have in common, besides me.

I left my home in Upstate New York at 16 to live in a barn in southern Maine for a marine biology internship, and I haven't stopped exploring since. My passion for wildlife led me to create my own YouTube-based wildlife series in 2004 and has landed me spots on Animal Planet, Nat Geo, Nat Geo Wild, Travel Channel, SyFy, BBC and more. Half of the TV shows I've made have never seen the light of day, but they were all an adventure and there isn't a single one I wouldn't do again if given the chance. Besides TV, I work full time in biotech, which is its own sort of adventure – albeit one where drinking the water is generally safer. I've been bitten and stung by just about everything you can think of – from rattlesnakes and black bears to bullet ants and a rabid raccoon – and I've lost count of the number of countries I've been to.

I've had the opportunity to travel the world interacting with some of the strangest and rarest animals while having the honor of living with indigenous peoples in some of the most remote locations – participating in their rituals, eating traditional meals, and massively embarrassing myself while always trying to remain respectful. I am a perpetual fish-out-of-water, even in my home state of Massachusetts. This book is part of the

"On the Hunt" series, in which I get to tell some of my favorite stories from those travels.

This particular book is about my time in Sumatra searching for the truth behind the mythical Orang Pendek, and bouncing around the country with my friends while making an episode of the National Geographic Channel series *Beast Hunter*, also called *Beast Man* in the UK, "Breast Hunter" by my wife, and "Beast Master" by almost everyone who meets me for the first time and tells me they enjoyed the series.

Sumatra is an incredible place – a place of unparalleled beauty, with wonderful people and amazing wildlife. I had some difficulties while I was there, but I love and respect the land, the people, and the animals, and feel privileged to have been able to experience it for myself. This shoot may have saved my life, and also threatened to end it on more than one occasion. Please take the attempts at humor in the following pages for what they are, and know that I mean no disrespect. I hope you enjoy this book. If you do, please pick up the others from this series. If you don't, I'll probably hear about why on social media. Either way, thanks for reading!

A disclaimer

My dog Daisy was the best. She loved hanging out in the backyard with my sister Sarah and me when we were playing hide-and-go-seek, catching bugs, or looking for arrowheads on the trails behind our house in Upstate NY. She would wait patiently at the base of any tree we climbed and chase away our neighbor's super scary dog (he ate a kitten once). She would also stand guard while I waited for the spider to crawl out of a crack in our chipped blue bulkhead cellar doors. It was huge, with green-metallic colored fur and red eyes, and Daisy would growl if I put my hand too close to it. She was a white poodle mix with poofy fur and perpetually muddy feet. Also, Daisy could fly, sometimes wore a cape, and would occasionally speak with a

Southern drawl.

I don't have schizophrenia and Daisy was not an imaginary friend – but she also didn't really exist. Despite never owning a dog as a child, I have honest, distinct memories of Daisy. Memories that go well beyond the stories my mom used to tell my sister and me about Daisy saving us from one tragedy or another. I also have detailed memories of being terrified, like heart-racing, nearly-in-tears fear the time Cookie Monster stole our shoes while we were wading in the creek catching crayfish and pollywogs. He would only give them back when we had the Count (who smelled like toothpaste) help us negotiate how many cookies it would take for each shoe, shoelace, and sock. Daisy ran back and forth from our house bringing with her a ransom of the ever-increasing number of chocolate chip cookies that my mom had left out to cool. The monster (I think people forget he is a monster by definition) kept finding loopholes in our deals, and the tension was getting higher and higher as the water rose in the creek. Cookie Monster smelled like BO and his eyes rolled around like a crazy person's. He was unstable. In the end, Daisy came through, as she always did.

Mom would start these stories, "When you were both very small, we had a wonderful dog named Daisy," and they quickly took on a life of their own. They eventually made their way into our collective consciousness as real events, complete with details not included in the original stories which must have been added by Sarah and me. It was years later, during some holiday involving drinking (see "every holiday"), that we started reminiscing about childhood memories and one of us asked: "Did we really have a dog when we were little? I kind of feel like we did, but I also can't picture us having a dog with all of the other animals we had. Daisy, maybe?" It wasn't until then that we realized these were, in fact, fictitious stories our mom had made up to keep us entertained on rainy days in our old house. Stories that drew on real events (being terrorized by a neighbor's dog, getting stuck in a creek, finding snakes, spiders, and arrowheads, etc.), with Daisy taking the place of our mother as the heroine.

I guess what I mean by this is, all of the stories in this book are exactly how I remember them, but I honestly remember having a flying southern-belle dog and interacting with Muppets. Take that how you want. I had a great childhood.

Oh, also – All views expressed are my own and do not reflect those of National Geographic, the National Geographic Channel, Icon Films, John Hunt Publishing, or any other person or organization mentioned (or not mentioned) in this book.

Chapter 1

Friends Don't Bite

In July 2010 I arrived in Java a little disheveled and tired, and completely unprepared for what the next two and a half weeks would bring. I was in Indonesia filming an investigation into Orang Pendek, the "short man of the forest" – a supposed species of tiny Bigfoot-like creatures that've been spotted on the vast chain of islands since time immemorial.

The flight was uneventful. A layover in Frankfurt provided the opportunity for some German beers, eating donuts while making the obligatory "Ich bin ein Berliner" jokes, and people-watching before a cloistered few weeks with the same four guys. Being that it was only 8am German time, the dimly lit, vinyl-seated, mirror-walled bar we were drinking in was empty aside from a frazzled-looking South American couple with an infant. They were arguing – or, more accurately, he was staring at the floor while she bounced the baby and quietly berated him in rapid Portuguese. Even without knowing the language, you could tell the husband was not pulling his weight during this important first international excursion with the baby. He was useless – he knew it, his wife knew it, and I'd have to believe even his child knew it. The woman left, possibly to reassess her choice of life partner, and the man proceeded to prop the baby into a wobbly standing position, hold one of its tiny little ineffectual hands as the only support, and turn away to watch soccer.

Twelve seconds later, as anyone observing could have predicted, the baby's legs collapsed under its own weight and his still pliable little skull hit the bar top to the general horror of all watching. A resounding, "Ohhhhhhh noooo," came from us, a much louder wail came from the child (after the horrific millisecond of silence in which babies turn their face into a grotesque old-man Halloween mask and stop breathing, prepping to let loose), and a completely terrified and muffled little, "Eyyy-ummmm-ahhhhhhhhh," came from the utterly clueless father. He confusedly picked up the screaming child and put him in a baby-carrier, strapping him in to prevent any future falls. The mom came back, asking the logical, "What the fuck?" as she walked in, to which the father shrugged and gestured, "No idea, he just started crying," and looked to our table for support. International "guy code", perhaps? We provided nothing of the sort, so he quickly made his only decisive action of the day, ushering his small family out of the bar before his partner could see the game on TV and put the pieces together.

After a few donuts and more than a few beers, we boarded the flight, stowed our overheads, and got our "in-flight" gear ready. Film crews and business people have flying down to an art. We are typically seen onboard with the barest of essentials, only those items that make 15-hour flights somewhat manageable. My one extravagance is a blow-up triangular monstrosity of a pillow. It rests on your lap and makes it super comfortable to sleep leaning forward on a crowded flight. You used to be able to find them in Skymall, now Amazon, but most people are too embarrassed to use them. Luckily, after 40+ years of nearly constant ridicule, I don't get embarrassed.

So we were prepped, the cabin door was closed, and we weren't moving. Ten minutes passed, then 20, then 30, until finally the pilot came on and said, "We have to wait another 35 minutes, we have no idea why and it would be pointless to ask us, so please do not." Gotta love the Germans. This would also basically sum up the next two weeks, although I didn't know it at the time: "We have no idea why this is happening, so don't ask."

Once in the air, the flight was unremarkable and relaxing.

About an hour before we landed, we were all handed customs declaration cards, standard for international travel. I checked mine off – yes, I certify I don't have any illegal drugs on me; no, I haven't used illegal drugs recently; no, there are no illegal drugs in my system; no, I haven't been in the presence of illegal drugs recently. "Wow," I thought, "Indonesia really cares about drugs." No, I'm not carrying more than 10,000 USD into the country, I have about $200 worth of goods that I plan on leaving in Indonesia, and then I reached a question I've never seen, and suddenly James, our sound technician, was at my side.

"Do you think they'll check my iPhone? I don't think they'll check my iPhone, right? Can they?" The statement on the custom form – "I certify that I am not bringing any pornographic material into the country" – was a new one for me, and apparently for James. I said my bet is that they won't check our phones, but any "German reading material" that may have been purchased in the Frankfurt airport should not leave the plane. James agreed and returned to his seat. There may have been something special in the seat back-pocket for the next lucky travelers.

We landed, joking about what may or may not be on our phones, and then realized that customs in Indonesia is no joke. The lines were pure chaos. People were screaming, guards were yelling and pointing, directing people haphazardly to one line or another. There were booths selling VISAs in case you "forgot to obtain one" for what appeared to be outrageous amounts of money, also with no guarantees that the VISA would be processed that day or that it would, in fact, serve as a VISA to get you into the country. There were also large, brightly-colored signs everywhere, stating, "If you have any trace amounts of any illegal drugs anywhere on your person, you will be killed." Not, "You will be arrested," not, "You will face prosecution," but, "You will be killed." And not one sign – lots of signs. Lots of big signs, in bright fluorescent colors reminiscent of eighties poster boards, everywhere, and in multiple languages. We glanced at each other and nervously made inappropriate jokes like, "I hope I washed my shoes after that party in St. Paul's," and "They can't mean heroin, right? Heroin must be fine if it's for personal use." But we were all sweating. A fine welcome to the country. It reminded me of getting off a plane in Costa Rica for the first time. After you get your luggage, you're funneled through this area with a life-size cutout of what appears to be a slightly overweight American businessman with a grin on his face and his hands in a "Hey now" kind of position. He has a word bubble coming out of his grinning toothy mouth that reads: "Pura Vida! Welcome to Costa Rica! Just a reminder, the age of consent is 18 in our country!"

We each chose a different line to wait in. The crew had a running bet on who could make it through customs the fastest based strictly on the appearance of the customs operative. Generally, I sought out a grandmotherly figure. I smile, say very little, act respectful, etc. Barny (series producer) and James chose young, attractive women – they are both incredibly handsome and naturally smooth. My experience is that this can backfire horribly, but they are both much cooler than me. Alex (2nd camera and associate producer) always tried to find someone who looked like a parent and usually played it slightly befuddled. Despite being 6'10", he can look like a lost child. Simon (main camera), possibly the toughest man I have ever met, would go for someone "who looks like they hate their life and could not care less about their job". As usual, Simon won on this occasion, but in a sad way.

We managed to make it through with our iPhones unchecked and our insane amounts of luggage arrived undamaged; and as an added bonus, no one was killed by the armed military guards for having partied a little too hard before leaving Bristol in England. It was then time to wait. One of the biggest misconceptions about filming is that it is nonstop adventure. In fact, there is a lot of stop. Everything is *crazy* busy – rushing, running, yelling, laughing – then stop, wait, sometimes for hours, sometimes days. A car has broken down, a camera won't work, we're picking up a plane on audio, we're picking up a dog on audio, we're picking up a goat on audio, the fixer has disappeared, the man you're supposed to interview has disappeared, there's a child picking their nose in the background, there's a man pooping in the background – lots of waiting. This time, we were waiting for our fixer. A fixer is a person who serves as translator, liaison to various governmental organizations, transporter, guide, and finder of meals and places to sleep. I love nearly every fixer I have ever met. It is a prerequisite for the job that they must be a person everyone likes hanging out with. There are some fixers that you *know* are ripping you off, but you still like them. There are fixers that love to treat you like a gullible tourist ("All locals drink horse semen! It makes you strong!"), only to crack under more questioning and bring you in on local secrets ("*Of COURSE* we don't drink horse semen! But it makes us laugh to see people try it!"). And you like them, even though they *just* tried to convince you to drink horse semen (true story). Fixers are also often responsible for your life, keeping you out of prison, cleaning up after any unintended and embarrassing *faux pas* you have made, and generally getting you everything you need in the short amount of time you spend in their amazing and often chaotic part of the world. They are the real heroes of all of my stories.

While waiting outside the airport I saw a man who looked, and was dressed, exactly like Kim Jong-il. That is not a look you achieve by accident. It's not something where you get a new haircut, shaved high on the sides, put on your freshly pressed grey-khaki jumpsuit, and throw on some absurdly oversized glasses, then catch yourself in the mirror as you're walking out the door and say, "Huh. I didn't really notice it before, but…" What was this man thinking? I kind of wanted to get into his head, but realized anyone who purposely tried to look as much like Kim Jong-il as possible was probably not a person I should approach in a strange airport. We took some obligatory photos in front of the "No pooping in the street" signs because we are 12-year-old boys. We were also approached by dozens of people selling "real American Rolexes" – which was funny on a few levels.

Our fixer showed up in a minivan that would make any soccer mom proud, and I immediately wanted him to be my Asian uncle. He was like an absurd parody of an Indonesian man – a tiny, round, balding, raunchy, sweaty, chain-smoking, little mustachioed man in a white suit. I could barely understand a word he said when he talked about anything other than how much money we owed him. He had a cooler full of beer (I genuinely loved him then) and "Pocari Sweat" drinks in the car. The first ingredient in Pocari Sweat was "air", so I figured it must be okay. When I went to open one, Uncle Jimmy – yes, my wish was granted when he said, "My name is Mr. Jimmy, but you can call me Uncle Jimmy," then hugged each of us – grabbed my wrist, looked me dead in the eyes, and told me I owed him $2, US. He then laughed like it was the best joke ever, then stopped, looked serious, and repeated, "$2, US," and wrote something in a little pocket notebook – most likely, "$5, US" – looked up, smiled, and hugged me again.

He talked nonstop on the way to our hotel, telling us he could get us "anything, anything you want. A Rolex? Real Rolex! Something better? ANYTHING!" It started to get a little weird, because I began to think he really meant it. As a general rule, I do everything I can to avoid spending time in a foreign prison, and no matter how many winks and nods I got from Uncle Jimmy I was not going to consider the possibility of a dual episode of *Beast Hunter* and *Locked Up Abroad*. The one thing I did want, which was perfectly legal although a little odd, was humanely sourced, cage-free Kopi luwak – the civet poo coffee.

Of course Uncle Jimmy could supply it! For an additional fee. He drove through the winding, overcrowded streets of Java to a hotel that he "had prepared special for us." He also promised a delicious meal that he "had prepared special for us," and again, "anything else we wanted," which, with its implications and his raised eyebrows, was definitely getting weird. The streets of Java are a writhing sea of vespas, dirt bikes, motorcycles, and amalgamations of the three best described as somewhat motorized, two-wheeled transport vehicles *laden* with goods, produce, and people. Yes, people – multiple individuals (sometimes entire families) on two wheels, oftentimes with goods *and* children in their arms. Steering can be done with any body part available. They careen in and out of what would be called lanes in the Western world, but here are barely guidelines. Miraculously, there are very few accidents, despite the *constant* sound of horns. Horns are used in Indonesia for communication, to make others aware of you, rather than to scream loudly at the Prius in front of you, as in the States. (I drive a Prius and am on the receiving end of a massive amount of Prius hate from the SUV and pickup driving population, though, of course, my car *is* fueled by childlike optimism and a sense of superiority so I kind of deserve it.) After the first of many stops at a government office to once again "confirm all of our paperwork is correct" (i.e. hand over money to Uncle Jimmy, who would turn over a portion of it to people in uniforms) we arrived at the hotel. It was probably 7 or 8pm and we were looking forward to that meal which had been "prepared special for us".

It turned out that, not only was there no special meal, there was in fact no hotel booked. A few phone calls back to England to the amazing, wonderful, patient, lovely, extremely talented, and very much asleep Anna at Icon Films, our production company, brought the truth to light that Uncle Jimmy had cancelled our room reservations, pocketed the money somehow, and failed in his attempt to rebook us in different, "special" accommodations.

James, Barny, and I were asked to wait in the lobby for three hours while "things get sorted". We periodically visited the misleadingly named "gift shop", which didn't sell souvenirs as much as toiletries and Western magazines – *Cosmopolitan, Time, Good Housekeeping,* etc. – hidden, black-boxed, and redacted as if they were porn. We did find that they had *Playboy,* but with no pictures – this was the only place where you could honestly say you were getting *Playboy* "for the articles". Just as we were starting to get a little frustrated it was announced that we had rooms and the promise of food by a slightly red-faced Alex, whose temper was just dissipating after a heated conversation with Anna, Uncle Jimmy, and the hotel staff. Icon had agreed to pay more than the original rate they had negotiated and would "work out the details" later to recoup the money Uncle Jimmy had pocketed. An unashamed and very enthusiastic Uncle Jimmy kept telling us how much better his deal would have been for us. Alex did not seem to agree, but the promise of food put us all in good spirits and we went upstairs with a young man who led us to our likely overpriced accommodations.

My room was pretty standard for *Beast Hunter* shoots – dubious sheets with a slightly greasy feel, rock-hard mattress, mold smell/visible mold in places on the wall, but a working AC unit! Four stars. What was missing, however, was toilet paper. By this point in my travel-filled life I was used to all types of bathrooms. I always carried my own TP and knew all about bidets, hoses, squat toilets, etc. Hotels were where I generally stocked up on toilet paper, and I was disappointed not to find any. I went to the lobby and found Uncle Jimmy. Here was his chance! Anything I want?, he wanted to know.

"How about toilet paper?"

"Toilet paper? What is that?" came his bewildered response.

Now – imagine me trying to mime toilet paper and its use to a very sweaty, very short, very mustached older Asian man. A crowd gathered – what does the large American want? Everyone starts guessing, like a cruel game of charades.

"Does he have crabs?" one man asks right off the bat. First question.

"No. Why would you jump right to that? No."

Does he need hemorrhoid cream? Are all of his 'parts' okay? Does he want an escort?

The questions keep rolling from equal-parts concerned and excited onlookers. Finally, an individually wrapped roll of TP was produced from behind the counter with the logo "TRENDY!" written across it. Ah, toilet paper! Of course! It's what all the kids want these days. It was one of only two rolls in the entire hotel. Alex was the lucky recipient of the second. Sometimes, I think about what they might have produced if it turned out that my "parts" were not okay, or if it was in fact body lice that was causing my distress.

Back in the room, trendy toilet paper in hand, I had 30 minutes before Uncle Jimmy's special meal. I enjoyed a quick shower (tepid water! 4½ stars!), attempted to use Wi-Fi (no such luck), and ritualistically separated my luggage into "going to need this all the time", "going to give this away to local kids", and "just in case". I was particularly proud of my travel bags for this trip – I had some new kit that I was hopeful would make life in the rainforest a little easier (it did not) and some extra food stashes that might come in handy later (they did).

Upon getting back down to the lobby it seemed Uncle Jimmy had left, but kindly prepared a table for us. In my experience, when the fixer opted out of eating with you, it was time to seriously lower your expectations for the meal. Some 2-3-day-old cold fish soup with congealed fat floating in it turned out to be the high point. The servers apologized and said they had not been expecting guests. We assured them it was not an issue, and we loved fish soup as we "enjoyed" our meal and discussed the next day's logistics. It seemed we would be given the rare treat of six hours of sleep! Breakfast and pack-out were early the next morning. We'd be heading off to Ragunan Zoo, where I would be working with an orangutan.

I am not an "Ugly American". I greatly enjoy and have enormous respect for local customs, traditions, culture, and food. I jump in with both feet, in fact. Splash vodka on your head before you drink, you say? Sure, I'm in! Blood clot soup? Seconds please! In fact, I'm really only disappointed when someone brings out a reheated hamburger which has clearly been in the freezer since the last American visitor some four years previous, and even then, only inwardly. I graciously thank the server for said meat patty and devour the hockey puck with fervor. The next morning's breakfast laid before us was something I had not expected based on the previous night. There was the same soup we had eaten the night before (we all were feeling distinctly unwell, except for James, who I believe could literally eat anything), still unrefrigerated, looking slightly slimier and thicker, but there was also chocolate cake (an odd but not unwelcome breakfast option), various fish products, steamed seafood, delicious juices, and Sumatran coffee!

I LOVE coffee. I've been drinking coffee since I was in a highchair and was overly excited for a cup of real Sumatran coffee in Indonesia – in Java, for God's sake. This was not good coffee, however. In fact, it was terrible coffee. The worst cup of coffee I have ever had. I am not unaccustomed to gut-rot, 2am, thick, tar-like, truck-stop coffee – this was… well, the only thing I can compare it to is grease or industrial lubricant, with lots of sugar in it. I was very sad for the people of Indonesia when I found out they export all of the good coffee and keep only the worst beans in their own country. Can you imagine growing the best tomatoes in the world but only ever eating the mushy, acidic, rotten ones? Also, sugar is a sign of wealth, so everything was covered in it – even the fish dishes and omelets which, in addition to being unpalatably sweet, had to be ordered "crispy" or they would be served essentially raw.

I eventually did have the best cup of coffee of my life in Sumatra. One of our guides had a good friend who owned a vegetable farm with a couple coffee trees – just enough for his own family. He served us a local spin on the treat dodol (normally a sugar-palm and rice flour-based candy, but here some boiled potatoes were also incorporated) and coffee, which we enjoyed in his living room with his family and his ox, who stuck its head and neck in the window for treats and to get its ears scratched. However, that first cup of lube-like coffee did things to my intestines that are not fit to print, but also woke me up and got me energized to film with the orangutan.

We were in Indonesia to look into the legends of the Orang Pendek (OP) – a "little bigfoot" or "hobbit" species of small, furry, ape-like men that supposedly inhabited the rainforests of Sumatra. I was heading to the zoo to film two known primate species that could be confused for OP in a classic mistaken identity scenario – the Orangutan and the Gibbon. It was possible we'd see both in the wild, but it was always good to have a backup plan to get the footage you needed. We needed close-up shots of both species to show how they move, how they walk, how they swing in the trees, etc., and the surest way to get that footage was at a zoo. As an added bonus, I had been cleared to interact with a captive orangutan – this would allow me to observe their behavior up close and see how they interacted with a human to compare this to the stories of human/OP interactions we'd be hearing in Sumatra. Also, any excuse to have me interacting with an animal – especially a dangerous or cute one, or in this case both – could lead to some great TV. It gave us promotional footage and images and filler shots, and helped to establish me as a wildlife biologist. There was also the chance that something would go awry and we'd get some dramatic shots of me being injured in some humiliating or terrifying way. Again, in this case – both!

I really enjoy working with primates, but they are hands

down the scariest animals on Earth. They are thinking creatures and, like people, are unpredictable. Anytime I get bitten by a snake I know exactly what I did wrong and it's 100% my fault. A chimp, though? Who knows? Maybe you reminded them of a person who shoved them when they were a baby, so they bite your finger off. Maybe they don't like the smell of the soap you used, so they defecate in your hair. They understand pain and it's why they attack your face and crotch first – they know it will hurt you the most. That alone is terrifying. I was working with a very young male chimp once, and he was being super cute, playing, doing flips, etc. Then he started peeing. He cupped his hand under the stream of urine and started collecting it. One of his trainers said, "He probably likes the warmth," but I wasn't sure; there was something in his eyes that told me that might not be the case. After a few more seconds of pee collection, he turned to a friend of mine whom I was filming with and, faster than any human could react, slapped him across the face with a handful of piss, hard, then fell over "laughing". I don't care what species you are, slapping someone in the face with a handful of pee is a fantastic insult.

We arrived at the zoo, went through the paperwork process again (this time, the fees took the form of a "mandatory donation" and a "guide fee") and started exploring. It was a big zoo, and I was excited to see a lot of species from SE Asia that I'd never seen in person before. As we were walking around we kept getting stopped by groups of people, mostly high-school kids, who wanted to take a picture with me. In other places of the world I've been this was pretty common as people aren't used to seeing Westerners, but here they kept saying things like, "I'm a very big fan of you," or "I really like you," or "You're very famous in your own country" – which I would try to correct them on, but they would just laugh at my attempts to dissuade them. I thought this was a little strange, but everyone was nice so I politely took pictures with all of them.

Uncle Jimmy kept saying, "I keep telling people you're very famous," but this didn't seem like it – people were asking for a picture *before* they spoke with Uncle Jimmy, and if anything they looked confused *after* talking to him. I thought maybe they really liked my webshow, *Nature Calls*. That was how I had gotten this job – maybe they had seen it? I tried to ask one of the groups how they knew me and the girls giggled and ran away after the picture, while one of the boys said, "You are very famous. We all love you." He was wearing a shirt that was covered in random English sayings in newspaper font – things like "Eat your vegetables every day", "I plead the fifth", and "I like to walk", but also "Go fuck yourself" and "bitch, please".

Another very polite kid who was probably 17 asked me how my music was. Confused, I said, "Great, I usually listen to punk rock but lately am getting into more singer/songwriter stuff?"

He seemed confused and just said, "*Your* music."

I replied, "Good, yeah," smiled, shook his hand, took a picture and said, "Thank you" – my standard response when I have no idea what's going on. Could he possibly know I was in a punk band in high school? Did people in Java somehow know who I was? After the 7th or 8th big group, I noticed Alex laughing. He was speaking with a young girl, who then came over and gave me a hug and took a selfie with me. Alex then told me she thought I was Chris Martin from Coldplay. James chimed in that some of the others thought I was David Beckham, he just didn't want to tell me because he wanted to see how long it would take me to develop an inflated ego. After that, I started really playing up the photos. I would pretend to be kicking a soccer ball (at least I thought I was, I have absolutely no idea what position Beckham plays or if what I was doing was similar to what anyone really playing soccer would do), or play air guitar – again, does Chris Martin play guitar? Well *this* Chris Martin does.

Simon was the cameraman on this shoot and he is, as I

mentioned, without a doubt the toughest man I have ever met. He was the main cameraman for Bear Grylls on *Man vs. Wild* and does everything Bear does, one-handed, with one eye closed and a 40 pound camera on his shoulder. There are Internet memes about Simon's toughness, and unlike the tales about Chuck Norris' tears (which would cure all diseases, but unfortunately he never cries), all of the memes about Simon are true. He looks younger than he is, with an angular, handsome face. He's not tall but not short and has a runner's physique. He is also an incredibly humble, kind, supremely talented, and quiet man who would stop to pet stray kittens and play games with children in between trekking up waterfalls and through waist-deep, disease-infested swamps. Anytime we couldn't find him for a few minutes we had a running joke that he was overthrowing the government of some oppressive regime, but he'd probably be back for tea.

The first stop in the zoo was to film some gibbons, which was great until one of them shat all over Simon. It perched above him as he was getting a gorgeous shot, then rained diarrhea on him, covering his head. We all laughed a little too hard, but when we saw that he had the shot (because Simon *always* gets the shot) we were impressed, and knew Gaddafi would be in trouble if Simon made his way to Libya. We helped him get cleaned up, asked him if Bear would have opened wide and drank it, then had some lunch of our own – Javan McDonald's. Slightly better than gibbon shit, and not the McDonald's menu you're probably familiar with. We had fried chicken, chili sauce, and rice as the Islamic call to prayer sounded over omnipresent loudspeakers followed immediately by Peter Cetera's 1986 hit song from *The Karate Kid Part II*, "Glory of Love," at equal volume.

Finally, we were ready for the orangutan. I was supposed to explain to the camera various orang mobility techniques – walking, brachiating, running, knuckle walking, etc., while the orang demonstrated them. I was then to compare what I was seeing to what the reports say of Orang Pendek's movements (upright, human-like, walking). Pretty straightforward. This was how most of our shoots for the series went – I was told what we were looking to accomplish, then given free range to give my thoughts and hypotheses. I would also describe the experiences to the camera. I didn't have "lines" or a script as much as an objective in each scene.

A zoo official dressed in a military-style green uniform and black boots brought us into the orangutan enclosure and went over all of the safety details: "Orangutans are very strong. Even as babies, they can kill you." I knew this, of course, but I listened politely, nodding my head. "They bite, tear, hit, rip – they can pull your arms off." Yup, another day at the office. "You'll be working with a seven-year-old female, Pinkie, she's just reached sexual maturity and really likes boys." My cutoff for working with great apes is generally sexual maturity. After that point, they are just too powerful and unpredictable, but this zookeeper assured me she was "very well behaved". "She will take a long time to warm up to you," he said. I told him I had worked with orangs before and knew a trick – make them come to you, pretend you found something really interesting when they're looking at you, and their natural curiosity will take over and they'll try to join in. The more you try to ignore them, the friendlier they will get. He said it was worth a shot, but warned me that if she got really interested she would "probably try to kiss me". I thought this would be great for the camera.

Pinkie was a little camera-shy at first. The zookeeper led her over to me, holding one of her outstretched hands. She looked like a curious toddler but, catching sight of the camera, ran away while continuing to glance over her shoulder at me. I sat on the ground and started intently playing with some grass – picking it up, staring at it, tossing it in the air, making it look interesting. She checked out what I was looking at, but wasn't impressed. I found some change in my pocket and started doing more of the same. When she came over to inspect I turned my back on her. She tried to look over my shoulder, so I hid the coins. She tried pulling my arms, so I held them firm. This was going exactly as I had hoped! Finally, I gave in and held her hand for a couple seconds. She was interested now – not in the coins (which I had discreetly pocketed again) but in this tall nearly hairless ape. Who was this new person in her home? She gave me a couple little kisses on the legs and head, then held my hand and walked with me. The crew was beaming. This was very cute, great footage. She brought me over to a little patch of trees, then noticed the camera and crew again and ran away. She kept looking at me though. This was all normal captive orangutan behavior, and it was going better than I expected.

While Pinkie was watching from a distance, an older female came over to investigate. This one had a scarred-over eye and an infant clinging to her. She walked up to me with no hesitation. This was a bold move for an orangutan, and one I hadn't experienced before. I didn't have to do anything to make her interested, she just walked, calm and collected, straight at me, staring me down, but looking interested, that light you always hear about very apparent behind her working eye. For some stupid reason, at that moment everything I knew about orangutans went out of my head. Everything had gone so well with Pinkie that I wasn't really thinking about how this one was older, had clearly had some trauma, probably human inflicted, had a baby with her, and wasn't the orang I had been cleared to interact with. Stupidly, so very stupidly, I reached out to her and grinned like an idiot, as if she was some friendly dog on a beach. Without flinching, she lunged at my hand, teeth first, and bit the air a few centimeters away from my fingers with a terrifying "knock" sound. Zookeepers rushed over, but I still had 10 fingers, for the moment at least. I realize now how ridiculously brainless all this was, but in the moment I just thought, "Oh, another friend! And you brought a baby," because sometimes I am truly that dumb.

Nearly losing a couple fingers did serve two purposes: it reminded me of a valuable lesson – namely, primates are the most terrifying animals on Earth – and it managed to get Pinkie's undivided attention. She was suddenly jealous. I was paying attention to another lady, one who apparently wanted parts of me to take with her. Pinkie walked over, grabbed my hand, and practically dragged me to another part of the enclosure (it was huge), as if to say, "This one is mine!" I tried doing a couple pieces to camera, talking about locomotion, the way she moved, etc. She kept interrupting and kissing or climbing me. She then climbed a tree and swung down to me – brachiating! I talked while she hung upside down and started tickling me. I was laughing and she was clearly enjoying herself, we were getting good footage even though I could barely finish a sentence – all was good.

Pinkie's kisses then started to get more aggressive, and her tickles turned into pinches. She was still upside down and suddenly I had an orangutan's arm all the way up my shirt, and she was pinching my nipple – HARD. Then she was back on the ground, kissing – nope, biting – my boots and legs. "Friends don't bite, Pinkie. We're friends, right? And friends DO NOT bite. No, no, Pinkie, that's not a tickle. Pinkie, friends don't bite! That kind of hurts, Pinkie!" I said, as her arm went up my shirt and grabbed my love handles hard enough to break the skin.

She proceeded to use those alarmingly long arms of hers to pull me into a bear hug and I realized just how strong she was. There was nothing I could do. She was completely in control. She was kissing my chest, then I saw teeth and she was making as if to bite my nipple off. She had ripped open my shirt and I was holding her head with both arms yelling, "Friends don't bite!", the only thing I could think to say in the moment, and pushing her away from me, but she was winning effortlessly. She had her feet wrapped around my waist, her arms around my torso, and my nipple was getting closer to her open mouth when two zookeepers rushed over and helped. Pinkie and I needed a little space.

While I caught my breath and the crew laughed hysterically (I don't blame them – as terrifying as it was, I could see the absurdity of it, and we *had* laughed at Simon, after all), Pinkie climbed up a little tree and waited for me. James tried approaching her and she spat on him and turned away. She was a one-man ape.

We still needed to get a lot of footage, so, after some time apart, Pinkie and I got back to it, and she didn't waste any time on foreplay. She hung by one foot and grabbed me with both hands and a foot, breaking the skin in multiple spots and tearing my shirt. Then she grabbed my crotch. It was a moment of sheer terror. All that was going through my head was the zookeeper saying, "They can rip your arms off," and I was thinking how the particular appendage she had grabbed was a little more sensitive than my arm, and probably easier to rip off. My thick canvas cargo pants somewhat cushioned the crushing force of her grip; however, there is a promo photo of this exact moment where you can see the outright horror on my face while Pinkie appears to be smiling. After that, I started trying to get away, but my God was she strong.

Next, she *rammed* her finger into my belly button, deep. If you have never had a child (or a primate) do this to you before, it is the oddest, most stomach-churning sensation. It hurts, nauseates, and tickles you at the same time. She did this a couple times and smelled her finger each time. I was sweating hard by this point, and on the last one she licked her finger, seeming to really enjoy it, then went for the nipple bite again. The zookeepers rushed in, and I looked to the crew who were still laughing. Barny shrugged and said, "This is great stuff! We need you to keep going," so we kept filming. She started grabbing my armpits and stomach, again drawing blood, then she reached down my pants, seeming to know there was something else that would be much more fun than my belly button.

Time froze for me, and suddenly there was a very rough, very elongated, but still human-like calloused hand with long fingernails down my pants, and inside my boxer briefs. My own hands were busy keeping her head away from my chest (which she was trying to bite again), and suddenly she touched my testicles – gracefully, thoughtfully, with one finger – then slapped them. Let me say that again – an orangutan caressed, and then *slapped*, my testicles – like she was trying to play a game of tetherball, and they would swing around my body.

I squealed in pain, and I'm not ashamed to admit it. It was a weird little noise that left my mouth. I let go of her head and grabbed her arm with both hands, no longer caring if she bit my chest as there were more important matters, like not letting her grab, squeeze, or tear off my testicles. She was completely engrossed in this new endeavor, and had found something much more exciting than my nipple. The crew was practically in tears now they were laughing so hard. After smelling her fingers and licking her nails, the hand plunged back down. There was absolutely nothing I could do. She yanked open my pants by the belt and peered down, intrigued like it was a grab bag and there were so many prizes to choose from.

After another glancing strike at my genitals, her probing fingers dove right past and, unfortunately for me, Pinkie lived up to her name. I felt a tough, leathery finger towards entirely new territory. She had reached up and under, and I felt her hairy arm brushing against my most sensitive body parts. I grabbed her arm with both of mine and pulled yelling, "Noooooope. No! Pinkie! Please don't do that! That's my butt!", and, as she curled her gnarled finger, fishhook-like, abruptly, like an alien abduction victim, I was probed. "Ayeee!" would best describe the noise I made. "NO, PINKIE!" She pulled her hand out, smelled her fingers, and seemed satisfied.

I had had enough. I turned, saw the crew staring open-mouthed, and I said, "Yeah, yup – that just happened," and walked away, awkwardly. Pinkie tried to hold my hand, but we were far past that by then. I was shaking, sweating, and disheveled. My lapel mic had come undone, my shirt and pants were torn, and my boxer briefs were bunched in a weird position. An orangutan had just performed a prostate exam on me. All in a day's work.

I was diagnosed with colon cancer a little while after the show finished, and one of my relatives swears that it was because of Pinkie. She knows that's not how cancer works – the vast majority of our family has had cancer, and I'm the only one (to the best of my knowledge) to have been violated by any nonhuman primate, but the whole experience seems so unusual and so unnatural that something horrible must have come from it in order for it to make any sense.

I left the zoo a little older and a little wiser. A more experienced biologist. A little more Beckham than Martin. When all was said and done, we got some great footage – none of which actually made it into the episode. We only used her knuckle walking alone, and her climbing down from a tree to claim me. To be fair, a show that *could* use footage of an orangutan violating somone would be a very different series than the one we were making, but it could have the same name – *Beast Man*, or *Beast Hunter*, actually.

Chapter 2

"You Smell Like Wet Death"

Think about the absolute worst, most torrential, biblical downpour you have ever experienced. Picture it in your mind, remember the rain blurring your vision, making it difficult to breathe without taking in mouthfuls of water, the sound filling your ears. Now double the amount of water, and imagine hiking and camping in it for over a week. You are now picturing my experience in Sumatra.

The trip started with me being violated by an orangutan in Java and went downhill from there. A couple days after the "Pinkie Incident", I woke in a shady hotel in rural Sumatra feeling distinctly unwell. My stomach was in knots and the cramps were making me a bit dizzy. While snuggled into my sleeping bag liner, lying on top of the thin, greasy sheets on my rock-hard bed, I turned on the TV and found that the power had come back on, having gone out for the third time in a day the previous evening. I was watching what appeared to be a talk show with a very campy, overweight Asian man wearing tons of makeup, hair product, and shiny tight-fitting clothes. He was "interviewing" – or more accurately yelling at – a group of teenage Asian boys who had the look of a boy band. I could spot the bad boy, the young one, the far-too-old one, the one who would be the first to start a solo career, etc. It was interesting to me that an Islamic country with a very draconian stance on homosexuality had so many over-the-top stereotypical gay men on TV. I was told that, in Indonesian entertainment, flamboyantly campy gay men are the most popular. After the boy band started singing what could have been *I Want It That Way*, I turned the TV off and made my way down to the veranda near a very cloudy and slimy-looking green pool.

I had a breakfast of green toast covered in condensed milk and rainbow sprinkles which, amazingly, did nothing to make me feel better. The green toast was interesting. I'm not entirely sure *why* it was green, but think it was supposed to be that color, and hadn't gone bad. Sticking with the theme of unexpected food colors, my coffee was nearly white from the amount of sweetened condensed milk, and a little crunchy from the insane amounts of added sugar. I felt a little better after drinking it – apparently, there is a tipping point when massive amounts of sugar in your system will make anything better.

I was dining that morning with James, who was bright and chipper as always (despite having only slept about three hours), and eating everything in front of him with relish. "Lovely place, isn't it?" said James staring at the murky water, sipping his off-white coffee. There was no hint of sarcasm in his voice. James is the most positive person I've ever met. He is five years younger than me, blonde haired, blue eyed, scruffy bearded, incredibly bright, has been everywhere and seen everything, and is nearly always in a fantastic mood. Basically, everyone at Icon is amazing, and some of the greatest, most-talented people I've ever come across, and even among this group of superhumans, James is a standout. This morning he was devouring a ramen-noodle omelet covered in an unknown blackish sauce, which he highly recommended, saying the only other option was a fried rice omelet, but he'd heard from our guides and fixers that the fried rice was simply refried rice leftover from other people's meals. I said I'd just stick with toast – which turned out to be the green, rainbow-sprinkled variety.

James had woken before the rest of the crew, as was his custom, sorting all of our kit and determining what we needed for filming that day. Every member of the crew is essential on every shoot, but realistically the "James" of the group is the most important. They are the person who does so many of the thankless but integral jobs – jobs you never think of until they aren't done, like charging the batteries, grabbing water purification tablets, and maintaining/fixing the equipment. He would be the last one to sleep and the first to wake up, the person who had all of the gear in their room/tent, and never complained.

Second only to the "James" of the shoot is the associate producer (AP). The AP works for months leading up to the shoot, sorting everything – every person you will meet, every car, plane, dugout canoe, and submarine you will be in. They fix the budget, sort the permits, haggle for prices, and keep the producer and host on track. They can often be heard saying: "I know, and that sounds brilliant, but we can't afford / don't have time / it isn't legal / can't put it on TV / has nothing to do with the story, so we need to move on. Here's a biscuit and some caffeine." Our AP on this shoot was Alex who, despite his aforementioned height, still looked like a little boy. All women find him "adorable", with his naturally tussled dark hair and ever-present crooked grin. He's just an all-round great guy as well – super talented, nice, funny, and thoughtful. His dedication to the crew made the rest of us feel lazy. Before seeing it, I couldn't have pictured Alex in a boat, but he's a natural and at ease with oars in his giant hands – which themselves could serve as passable oars. By this point, I had gotten used to being the most useless person on any shoot. I have no patience for any host who acts like "The Talent" – which is what our contracts read, despite the fact that we clearly have the least amount of talent on any shoot, and most of us know it.

James told me he had met a lovely Chinese couple at the hotel who were doctors visiting Sumatra on a humanitarian mission: "The man said he was going for a swim. I tried to warn him and his partner seemed uneasy about it, but he insisted he'd be fine. He jumped in, swam a lap or two, and got out. He smelled VERY strange after his swim. Not bad, but strange."

I could see the draw of a pool – it was oppressively hot and humid, after all – just not *this* pool. The hotel had a sort of "gone to seed" luster to it. You could tell it was once great – huge columns at the entrance, a grand pool, a massive outdoor dining space looking out at a cloud-capped, rain-forested mountain. It was beautiful, even if it seemed no work had been done on it since the early seventies. Almost everything was broken or in the process of breaking: the doors were warped by the humidity and had a slimy feel, the locks were broken and rusted, the AC units smelled of damp and rattled, water dripped from faucets and spurted at odd angles from shower heads, and the pool chairs were a mixed bag of mismatched materials and tetanus-introducing rusted metal. There also seemed to be a constant battle to keep the mold at bay all over the hotel, with neither side conceding. The pool was clearly losing, though, and I had to agree with James – taking a dip did not seem like a good idea.

The rest of the crew joined us for ramen omelets and also denounced the decision of the nice young doctor. As we had a packed agenda and I wasn't feeling any worse than I had when I woke up, we were off. The car ride was your average white-knuckle journey over broken pavement and dirt roads, and through mopeds manned by very young children carrying their still younger siblings in one arm. Besides the two-wheeled monstrosities that dominate the streets of Java, in Sumatra you'll find the majority of cars to be what James called "Fun Buses". These are brightly-colored, souped-up, VW bus-style vehicles. Most, interestingly, had American cartoon characters painted on them and random strings of English words like "Sugar Table Slut Dollar" (my personal favorite). Many of them had massive speakers, some with the minivan-style sliding door removed to best share their music (and allow occupants to lean out at high speeds), which was a surprising mix of nineties American hip-hop and cheesy Indonesian love songs. It was a little disorienting to see a purple van covered in images of Donald and Daisy Duck, with the words "Bitch Weed Street Cash Valley Maple" stenciled on the side, filled with eight young Indonesian men, pass you as you hear Coolio rhyme the lyrics to his 1995 hit *Gangsta's Paradise* and it's 2010. I began feeling worse the more we drove and decided to lie down in the back of the van. James (who also served as our pharmacist) gave me tablets of some stomach-easing powder and some electrolytes, and suggested I spend time on the squat toilet in the near future – "better out than in" was a motto amongst the crew.

Two hours later, while eating mystery meat at an outdoor table in the back of a restaurant in town, I discovered the meaning of the term "violently ill". I found myself writhing on the ground in stomach-churning agony with the worst gastrointestinal pain I had experienced. I was vomiting from the pain, nearly blacking out, and contorting my body while lying on pillows that the crew had placed on a dais in the restaurant's back garden. This description – "dais in the back garden" – conveys more of a sense of beauty than it deserves. Yes, it was technically a "dais", being a raised platform, but its state of repair was in keeping with everything back at our hotel, and I appeared not to have been the first person to vomit on it recently. And yes – it was a "back garden", in that it was a garden behind the restaurant, but again, and not to belabor the point, I don't want you imaging a picturesque, serene, SE Asian paradise. This was more a backlot that smelled of cigarettes and diesel and was oppressively hot and humid, with the sounds of traffic filling the air, intermingled with my grunts of pain.

The waves of pain would come about every 10 minutes and last for about two. For the remaining eight I would catch my breath and assure the wait staff that a massage would definitely not make me feel any better, but thank you for offering. There was a suggestion that I should go to a hospital, but our fixer in Sumatra – a British man who had lived in the country for years – strongly advised against it, saying, "Mate, out this far into the country, I'd rather deal with whatever you've got than what they might give you," so the pain kept coming. Gradually, the time intervals between the pain increased and the pain of the episodes decreased to the point where it only felt like bad cramps every hour or so. I was offered more massages, given a lot of Pocari Sweat drink, and then – well, we had a lot of filming to do and had lost almost an entire day, so we got back to work. I didn't 100% recover, the following month was particularly nasty, and I was eventually diagnosed with stage three colon cancer – but that's another story.

The crew decided I must be pregnant and started referring to the incident as "when Pat was in labor". There were a lot of jokes about how surprised Anna (now my wife, then my girlfriend) would be when I got home. Would I name the baby after them? They thought I'd been putting on some weight, but didn't want to say anything. Now it made sense why I was eating such bizarre foods. Could Pinkie be the father? It's awesome having a crew of all guys.

Anna will get a lot of mentions from here on out, so it's best to introduce her properly. We met in 1999 at Suffolk University in Boston, Massachusetts when she was a freshman and I was a sophomore. I will never forget the first time I saw her, as it was the only time in my life I have been left literally speechless by a woman I've never spoken to. She was in a dress on her way out for the night, and I was in some dirty army pants and an old Ramones T-shirt hanging out in the cafeteria. I pretended to study the overhead menu for the entire duration she was in line and made awkward eye contact a few times, but was physically unable to speak. She was probably (rightfully) weirded out by me. She made her exit, I regained my ability to function, and I told my friends that the most attractive woman I'd ever seen had just walked out of the room.

I figured out who she was a few weeks later when it turned out that I'd be the Teaching Assistant in her intro to chem lab. I spent the next few years getting to know her – teaching a couple of her labs, assisting the teacher in others, hanging out occasionally as friends, selling her my old books. Any excuse to talk to her. I literally wrote things down to say to her the night before our labs together, then lost my nerve and just talked about the subject matter at hand, or her trip to Vietnam when she was 14 (my go-to "Hey, I know a fact about you!" bullshit discussion). I sat awkwardly on my lab stool flicking my gloves against my thumb to make them "pop" and stared off in space, because I'm super cool like that. I finally got the courage to ask her out on a date at the start of my senior year. She had transferred to a different university in Boston and we were both single, and to my amazement she said yes. Our first date was at the New England Aquarium – which is the most Pat Spain thing to do, ever – and it was closed – which is actually *the* most Pat Spain thing to do, ever. We then went to a nice Italian restaurant, and when I tried being classy and asked if we should order some wine she looked really nervous, and said, "Ummmm... I better not."

To which I replied: "Oh, I just thought wine might be nice. I'm not trying to get you drunk and take advantage of you or anything." Those words actually left my mouth.

She just said: "I mean, I'm only 20..." For those of you not in the States, the drinking age here is 21, and Anna was only trying to avoid an awkward situation of not being able to produce valid ID to get a drink, so of course, I created a *much* more awkward situation. She married me. I still don't know how or why.

Anna is 5'3" and fiercer and more loyal than anyone you could meet. She's first-generation Vietnamese and grew up in Lowell, Massachusetts, former Crack Capital of America, which, if she's been drinking, she will usually tell you in the form of a shouted, "I'm from LOWELL," and an implied, "Don't fuck with me or my family" – sometimes it's not "implied" so much as "implicitly stated". She's amazing in every way – an amazing mom, funny, kind, and supersmart (she destroyed me in organic and all other chem classes, overall Grade Point Average, and, you know, life). She would have been totally fine if I'd come home and told her I was pregnant – if that was physiologically possible.

We decided to film the market scenes in Sungai Penuh next as they didn't require me to do all that much. If you've never been to an open-air market in a developing country, you're really missing out on one of the more easily accessible life-altering experiences. It's hard to look at commerce or produce in the same way after seeing men and women so skilled at their particular trade that their musculature has actually adapted to it – their very body altering to better suit it. A man crushing peppers on an ancient mortar and pestle, with his shoulder and forearm muscles on the crushing arm dwarfing those of his somehow elongated gripping arm, his nails dyed red from the paste he scrapes, his eyes immune to the pungent fumes. A woman with actual grooves in her hands that serve as guides for the yarn she weaves – it's intense. If you have sensory integration disorder or just get overwhelmed easily, then stay away. Most markets are pretty similar in that they contain far too many people and animals (alive and dead) in far too small a space. Lots of shouting, lots of sweat, tons of smells, random vehicles, and treasures you didn't even know you were looking for. For a person who has always collected random assortments of bizarre crap, these markets are my mecca and the bane of my very organized, practical, and minimalist wife. "We really don't need another statue / demon repellent / preserved animal part – why don't you buy a fridge magnet? Or something to hang on the wall?"

The first thing you notice as you approach the market is an overpowering smell, usually a pungent mix of diesel, BO, cigarettes, rotten vegetables, and fish. This one had the unexpected added bonus of chili peppers – in fact, in some places, the air hurt to breathe and made your eyes sting, all of which was perfect for an already upset stomach.

I was here to ask people what they knew about Orang Pendek, or if they could direct me to anyone who knew about the creatures. I was also supposed to buy some supplies for the trip – I had a "to buy" list, in a language I couldn't read, and some idea of basic ingredients/materials to provide (bribe) officials with. Kreteks were a favorite – tobacco cigarettes with cloves mixed in so they crackle and pop as they burn, and smell and taste sweet. The majority of the population appeared to chain-smoke them. At one point during the trip, the road we were traveling on was washed out and we needed to make a midnight stop at a stranger's house, who let us sleep on his kitchen floor and cooked us breakfast. He and some of our local fixers stayed up until 5am drinking, laughing, and smoking kreteks about two feet from us. I must have inhaled the equivalent of a pack that night, and to this day my sleeping bag smells like a lame art student's dorm room.

I spoke with a few people at the market and made them laugh with my terrible Indonesian. I am horrible at languages. Anna and I have been together for over 20 years, and all I've learned to say in Vietnamese are food words and swears. Whenever I try to say, "Thank you," I say, "Salty fish." This would have actually come in handy here because one of the things I needed to buy was salty fish. When trying to learn a new language, I generally start with "hello", "thank you", "I need a doctor" and various food and bathroom words. The swearing is an added bonus, and I learned that the top insult in Indonesia roughly translates to "I can buy your soul", which is way meaner than "Fuck you" when you think about it. I managed to buy veggies, cigarettes, fish, meat, some dodol, spices, chili peppers, and rice. I also made a lot of locals laugh and probably became the butt of a bunch of jokes because word soon spread that I was looking for "short men". "Orang Pendek" literally translated means "short man". Everyone wanted to see the tall American who was asking around for short dudes. One older woman pointed and said, "Look around! All of these men are short! You can have your pick, take any of them." Another grabbed her dejected, bashful, blushing husband and said, "This is my short man! You can't have him." Then, with a wink and a devious smile, slapped his butt. It was very clear that the ladies ran this market. I noticed that *they* were the ones yelling and gossiping, bossing around the men, and even making catcalls at the shirtless delivery boys. This was a fairly conservative Islamic country I was in, right?

Yes, most of the women wore headscarves, but they also made very dirty jokes and grabbed my butt when we posed for pictures. One of my favorite moments at the market came when a hunched over, near-toothless older woman in a black headscarf saw Alex, big Alex, who would be considered tall on an NBA team, and ran out of her stall screaming. She was so excited! She hugged him, face at crotch height, and kept slapping his legs, laughing hysterically. She then picked up various phallic vegetables and started waving them at him, to the general amusement of everyone around us. She kept asking a question, answering it herself, then grabbing a new veggie. Finally, she got to an eggplant that must have been a foot and half long and seemed to appraise Alex, then announced something loudly in Indonesian, handed the eggplant to him, laughed hysterically, and squeezed him again. Our translator was practically on the ground laughing. He translated for us:

"Wow, wow, wow, wow, this man must have the biggest penis on Earth! Is it this big? No, no, much bigger! This big? No, look at him! That face, those hands, those FEET! It must be huge! Ladies, how big? THIS big? No, he is so handsome, and such a huge penis! It must be this big! (handing him the eggplant). Yes, I think that looks about right. Ladies, take a picture and remember this day! Oh, I wish I could bring you home."

Alex, incidentally, gets this question more often than you would guess, just usually less explicitly and generally a little more drunkenly. His standard response is: "Proportionally, I should be a foot taller."

By the time we left the market I was feeling a little better, but not quite well enough to head into the jungle and start our search for OP in earnest. Luckily, Sumatran bureaucracy gave me a little break. We had been planning an intense hike into a national forest about two days from the nearest dirt road – to an area that had frequent and fairly recent OP sightings. We would set up camp and a bunch of camera traps and pheromone lures, and hope we got lucky with a photo or sighting. We'd also hike all around, showing OP's habitat and ecosystem. This seemed straightforward and manageable, until taking into account underpaid and power-hungry government officials. Long Tall Alex (as he will forever be known) met with a small man (but then again, everyone is a small man compared to Alex) in a military uniform for over three hours without making any progress. We had all of our paperwork, had all of it signed, co-signed, and faxed to every office it needed to go to, stamped, and in a neat binder marked "permits". This civil servant, however, decided that we needed a copy for everyone in the office that day, and they did not have a working copy machine or printer. Alex spent another few hours cruising rural Sumatra looking for either of these two signs of the modern world. He finally found a copy machine in the back of a convenience store, and any logical person would conclude we were now good to go. Unfortunately, despite telling Alex they would wait, the government officials closed their offices early that day, and we would need to wait until the next day to turn our forms in.

While Alex was making friends with the local government we headed back to the hotel. In the lobby we saw the nice doctor couple again. The man was hunched in a corner looking about the same shade of green as the toast I had eaten that morning while the woman was speaking, calmly but firmly – very like a doctor – to the staff of the hotel. She was telling them exactly why it was so important to chlorinate a standing body of freshwater in this environment, and listed some of the multitudes of microbes the man may have contracted. He slumped into a heap as she said, "but he really should have known better," and glared at him with a fantastic and unmistakable "stupid man" look. They were leaving not just the hotel, but the country. Apparently, they had seen the nearest hospital and would rather wait until they got home. Later that night we saw the very confused-looking staff dumping massive amounts of chemicals (all different kinds) into the pool. By morning it looked like everything in the pool was dead, and smelled like anything or anyone who went in would also die.

Bright and early the next day, Alex was at the door of the government offices, forms in hand. The officer from the day before was not there, and the new officer needed everything explained to him again, causing another three-hour delay. Alex left in a rage like I have never seen after being told they would review the forms and call us when they were done. Twice that day Alex had to go back to the office as "the conversation could not occur over the phone", nor could he wait at the offices while they reviewed his answers, and they needed him to explain why we did or did not have a form, pay some very dubious "fee" for additional permits, meet with the Indonesian National Armed Forces (he said he would have been terrified if he wasn't so angry), and hire a "government escort" who would "explain and open the beauty of Sumatra's national parks to us on our excursion". It turned out that this "guide" hated the jungle, had never been to the park we were going to, refused to carry any of his own equipment, barely left his tent, and smoked all of our porter's (and real guide) kreteks. The one contribution he made was, one night around the campfire, saying, "I've seen Orang Pendek." When I asked him to explain he replied, "Just kidding," and laughed, his crooked, stained teeth prominently displayed. For this he demanded extra pay for "being part of the show".

Finally, we got our permits. We had the government's permission, we had our guides, porters, supplies, and eyewitnesses lined up, the random government official in tow, and gear, and were ready to leave the chaos of the village of Ulu Jernih, where we had been staying while Alex ventured into town to deal with the government, and enter the bizarre and untouched world of Kerinci Seblat National Park. We started the hike in bright and beautiful sunshine. Farmers worked in rice paddies on the side of the dirt road, water buffalo pulled equipment as they have for hundreds of years, and folks came out of their homes to wave and cheer to us as we walked by. It was gorgeous – every scene looked like a postcard or a cutaway from some travel channel food show. We reached the end of the dirt road where it turned into farmland. A farm had been built on the side of the mountain and marked the entrance to the forest, and beyond a field of chili peppers we saw only tall forest canopy heading up a steep incline. We were all in good spirits after the beautiful walk and my stomachache was feeling a little more manageable. We started climbing the side of what I later found out was an active volcano, Gunung Tujuh. It was steeper than it looked, and we needed to grab roots and tree trunks in places to get up the muddy, overgrown path. After about two hours we stopped seeing any traces of people – no cigarette butts, Pocari Sweat bottles, or even boot prints. The guides told us very few hunters went beyond here and advised us to keep an eye out for tigers. (A few nights later, in the forest, we were stalked by a tiger. A few of us saw it about 30 feet away, watching us. One guide told us not to worry too much: "The tigers in Kerinci Seblat are very polite." This was good to hear, as an impolite tiger sounds like trouble.)

About an hour after spotting the last cigarette butt it started to rain. Shortly after that, I came to the understanding that I had never really known rain up until this point in my life. This rain was intense, and we were climbing an increasingly steep, jungle-covered volcano in it. Over slippery roots, up muddy slopes, and over fallen trees we went, heavy packs on our backs throwing off our balance. James and Simon had it the worst as we were filming while hiking. This meant Simon needed his pack and camera, and James his pack and all the sound equipment. James wore a massive utility belt that would have made Batman proud and huge headphones. He had wires and metal sticking out at odd angles all over his body, and a poncho attempting to keep things as dry as possible. The three of us often had to double-back and hike the same ground we had just climbed if there was a good shot to be had. Anything I grabbed to steady myself seemed to be covered in thorns or stinging nettles. There were also periodic earthquakes, each bringing our progress to a nervous standstill. Did I mention we were on an active volcano? Iceland's Eyjafjallajökull volcano had unexpectedly erupted a few months before this, and the resulting ash brought air travel to a standstill (we were in Cameroon at the time), while a short time before that Sumatra had experienced its worst earthquake and tsunami in recent memory, and we had visited the still-destroyed epicenter. You could smell the bodies under the rubble where rescuers had not been able to move the collapsed buildings. You couldn't help but let your mind turn to these images. There are so many things that can kill you on a shoot in these locations. You can try your best to account for many of them, but earthquakes? Tsunamis? Volcanoes? They bring it all to a new level.

After about six hours of near-vertical climbing, and having basically climbed the volcano twice due to doubling back to film, we crested the top just as the sun poked out. We were treated to a view of old-growth rainforest all around us. It was gorgeous. Even as exhausted, soaked through, sick, and muddy as I was, I could not deny how incredible this place was and how lucky we were to be seeing it. It was also pretty clear why this volcano was not in any *Lonely Planet* travel guides, despite its majesty. I spotted a fantastic euarchonta (tree shrew), a representative of the order of mammals that spawned lemurs and the great apes, including us. Some of the guides found a mildly venomous snake and I was excited to handle my first reptile in Sumatra. I was just starting to catch my breath, and we had stopped for some snacks and to dump the water out of our boots, when the rain started again, just as hard as before.

The daylight was fading as we made the descent into the mouth of the volcano. Although the volcano was technically active, there has been a lake in it for hundreds, maybe thousands, of years, and, aside from the rumbles and occasional geysers (which we did not see), there was really no volcanic activity to speak of. The hike down was less dramatic than the hike up. Maybe it was exhaustion or maybe it was our inexplicable ability to acclimate to the new, but despite the constant downpour, continuing earthquakes, snakes, slips, falls, cuts, bruises, and thorns, the hike down was utterly unremarkable.

We reached the lake in the dark, and the guides advised us it would be unwise to cross at night. We were already a couple of days behind schedule, but Barny, our fearless leader, made the call to play it safe. We'd set up camp and leave at dawn. We erected tents and changed out of soaking wet clothes, only to realize we didn't have dry clothes to change into. All of our bags had soaked through. Our war-tested, well-used, and generally reliable waterproof outer shells were no match for Sumatra's relentless rain. It honestly would have been like taking your pack, submerging it in a lake, and pushing on it for six hours. Nothing could stay dry in those conditions. We camped that first night, soaked to the bone, on the shores of a volcanic lake that we could barely see. I slept like a baby, despite the rain outside, the rats jumping on my tent and head, and being in a soggy sleeping bag while continuing to deal with stomach issues.

I woke up just after dawn, refreshed and surprised at my own optimism, and ready for the rest of the hike. I put on my soaking wet clothes and left the tent. It had stopped raining just before dawn and I found myself standing in one of the most gorgeous spots I have ever seen as the sun rose over the distant mountains. The lake was massive and crystal clear, and steam billowed from its surface. It was surrounded by jungle, there was a waterfall just to my left, and you couldn't see the far side. Clouds rolled over the mountaintops that enclosed the lake and shot back up after almost hitting the water. It looked like a rainforest that a little kid would draw which, after visiting many tropical places, you resign yourself to the sad fact of this epitome of "rainforest-ness" not actually existing. But it does in Sumatra. I'll let you decide if you want to see it badly enough to go there after reading this.

We shot a bunch of production stills that morning and used water from the waterfall to make coffee and cook rice and fish. I caught a couple endemic (meaning they are only found in one specific region) lizards and frogs, and was really getting excited, when my stomach did a flip. Maybe the salty fish had pushed my already compromised system a little too far. I rushed away, barely making it past James' tent before squatting and doing what needed to be done. James, accidently happening upon the scene when he was looking for his own bathroom, described it as a "crime against humanity", and insisted, "They'll try you in The Hague for that, they will."

Our first order of business, once we were up and going, was to get across the lake in tiny, thin, ancient-looking and unstable dugout canoes called sampans. In a sampan you actually ride below the water level with the highest point of the canoe about an inch above the surface. Jeremy Holden, one of our guides, was unfazed by nearly everything. He drank the water, untreated, from streams, grabbed snakes and *then* identified them, wandered around alone at night knowing there were tigers in the area, and generally appeared to be a total bad ass. Jeremy told me that he was scared of the boats, having nearly died in them twice. Apparently, they tip really easily. It was not very confidence building to have Jeremy say he was scared of something. They are dangerous under the best of conditions, and this was not the best of conditions. We weren't on the water for 10 minutes (it's a 2.5 hour trip) when the rain started again. At that altitude, the temperature drops fast. The canoes were filling with rainwater and most had small cracks which let lake water in, so they needed to be bailed out constantly to prevent them from sinking. However, the bailing caused them to tip and allow water to come in from one side or the other. It was a losing battle. I was sitting in a couple inches of water, shivering, freezing, in a downpour. About an hour later, hypothermia began setting in. I was in my all-cotton (a stupid mistake on my part) TV uniform as we filmed the crossing, with all of my waterproofs tucked away in my soaking-wet bag on another boat. About twenty minutes after I started shaking, we had to pull the sampan over to the shore, get me wrapped in a space blanket and let me run in place until I was no longer uncontrollably shaking and turning blue, and then hop back in the boat for the rest of the trip.

I arrived at camp angry, sick, exhausted, and soaked. It was a bonus to find that my bag had actually been underwater for most of the trip, so my clothes and sleeping bag were not so much "wet" as "completely waterlogged". I would not be entirely dry again until my plane landed in England more than a week later. Before that, though, we had an investigation to do. We set up camp, cursing and exhausted – except James, who was as enthusiastically happy as always – and sat down for a meal of curry tuna and sardines. Just the thing for an upset stomach.

We then realized that Simon was nowhere in sight, and in fact we hadn't seen him for about 45 minutes since he had said he was going to set up camp a little out of the way rather than on the bank of the lake like us. On shoots in locations like this – if someone is out of earshot for longer than it takes to poop, you get worried. Simon is not just "someone" though. This guy knows his stuff. He didn't just "set-up camp", he went all "man vs. wild". He said that, after years of watching Bear do all of the "fun stuff", he wanted a shot at it. He had used his bowie knife to cut down some massive bamboo shoots and erected an enclosed hammock-like sleeping area from palm fronds, bamboo stalks, and other leaves. It was impressive, and even more so when we realized it worked better than our tents at keeping water out. He had also gathered some fruit that he thought "looked edible" and found a stream with fast-moving water for us to drink not too far from the camp.

The next week consisted of hikes through knee-deep mud just to get to the area of the forest we used as a bathroom, hikes in thigh-deep mud and thorns to get to areas pertinent to our search, and leeches, so many leeches, all while the rain continued in torrents. There is a piece of footage of us sitting under a tarp, cooking some crabs from the lake. James is grinning maniacally and Alex is filming:

Alex: "What's going on, James?"

James, grinning: "It's raining."

Alex: "How long's it been raining, James?"

James: "Forever."

Alex: "When's it going to stop raining, James?"

James: "Never! HA, ha, haha."

That about sums it up. We were all slap-happy. We were going to sleep wet, in wet sleeping bags, waking up and putting on wet clothes. We pulled leeches off ourselves daily. When you squatted to poop you could see them sliding towards your ass, and that is not at all an exaggeration – the second you stopped moving and looked around you could see leeches making their way towards you from all directions. We created a path that split into three different paths and left a stick at the split which served two purposes: 1 – if it was there, you knew no one was pooping down any of the paths, and were clear to proceed; if it was gone, someone had grabbed it and was using it to – 2 – dig a hole, steady themselves as they squatted over the hole, kill the leeches as they crawled towards them, and then bury what they'd left behind in the hole. (Okay, that's more than two things, but "multi-purpose stick" sounds weird.) I learned the etymology of the term "wrong end of the stick" that week when I found it lying on its side and did not feel well enough to do the "sniff test" before picking it up. I also pulled a leech off my testicles one day and momentarily lost my mind – like that scene in *Stand by Me*, but with less Corey Feldman.

Most of the porters and guides stayed at camp while we were in the jungle shooting. They gathered food, cooked, and found cool animals for me. I started noticing that they avoided Alex, leaving the main tarp area whenever he got there. Some of them wouldn't even look at him. I couldn't figure out why – they were all nice guys, Alex is an amazing guy, so what was the issue? I asked Jeremy (who is fluent in nearly every SE Asian language), and he said, "It's because he's a giant," totally seriously. I laughed, but, Alex really *is* a giant, legally. In England he qualifies for government assistance to buy clothes because of his height. This fact will always be hysterical to me.

One day the guys had made an amazing curried fish, and Alex was saying how excellent it was. They looked afraid. Alex asked if he could please have seconds and you would have thought he had pointed a gun at them. They jumped and started yelling and rushed to refill his bowl, practically tripping over each other in their haste. Jeremy started laughing and translated what they'd said: "Quick! The giant requires more food!" They actually thought he ate people and might eat them if he got too hungry, though this could have been partially my fault. I've mentioned my complete lack of language skills – at one point, I tried complimenting one of our guides who had cooked dinner and accidently said, "I eat children. Delicious!" He was completely silent, so we tried to change the subject and Alex asked where we could find the "People of the Inner Forest" – a tribe we were looking for – but instead asked where we could find the "people with tasty insides". They looked at both of us a little crooked after that.

Language skills have never really been my thing. I barely passed basic Spanish in junior high. It was far and away my worst subject. In fact, I only managed to pass my oral exam by remembering the word for fish – pescado – and using it in every answer:

"What will do on your weekend in Spain?"

"Fish."

"Okay, I guess that technically works. What are you most looking forward to in your excursion to downtown Barcelona?"

"Fish."

"Once again, technically, yes, there is a fish market in downtown Barcelona. What will you bring back to your friends in the US?"

"Fish."

"Mr. Spain, you're really stretching it here, but are technically not incorrect."

"Fish?"

When my teacher commented that my "corbata looked askew" after the exam, I replied, in shocked indignation, that it was very inappropriate for her to be looking at my corbata at all. Yes, my language skills had the potential to get me detention or a bad grade up until this point in my life, but now they could get us into some shit. Luckily, most people laughed at my butchering of the language. It became a running joke throughout the series. "Thank you" in Indonesian is "terima kasih", except when I said it, it sounded like "terrible coffee". In Thai, "thank you" is "Kob Kan Man", or "cucumber" for me. After attempting to order in French at a restaurant in Paris, a waiter offered, in English, "I have a deal for you, yes? If you stop destroying my language, I will speak in English." It was a good deal, and I took it.

After a few days in the forest I took my boots off and realized I was developing trench foot, a condition where layers of skin rot off from never drying out. I also had diaper rash from my soaking pants, and mold growing on the shirt I was wearing along with the spares in my bag. We had hiked up waterfalls, into untouched rainforest and thorn-filled swamps, and through the absolute harshest, most unforgiving landscape I have ever experienced. We went through bat caves where we were constantly urinated and defecated on from above, it fell like a light mist, covering us in unknown viruses. We waded, almost chest deep, through snake, leech, and disease-infested water that was so filled with bat urine and feces that it burned your nose to smell it. It was, without a doubt, the most uncomfortable I have ever been, and that's saying something. All of that being said, though, it was remarkable.

The rainforest in Sumatra is one of the most gorgeous places on Earth. It is honestly like a movie set – it doesn't look real, and you keep asking yourself whether it is. There was a mountain near our camp that our guide said that, to the best of his knowledge, not even a dozen people had climbed, and another where he thinks he was the only person to have ever summited – not "only Westerner", but only person. The locals really didn't come to this area because the terrain was rough, there wasn't great hunting, and there were some superstitions that kept people away. We climbed the first mountain and it truly looked like the land that time forgot. It was covered in moss nearly two feet thick. I kept expecting hobbits or orcs to crawl out of the caves. We kept our eyes (and noses) out for any signs of an *Amorphophallus titanum* (literally, "the giant misshapen penis") – a massive corpse flower so named for its appearance and odor. Depending on where your tastes lie, we were either lucky or unlucky to not encounter a plant that looks like a six foot phallus and smells like a rotting corpse, but we did see a lot of weird flora and fauna. I caught animals that are only found in one region of one tiny island, and plants that are only found in one little patch of land on one mountain in the entire world! I saw a truly unexplored wilderness, and learned firsthand why researchers are not cataloging new species all the time in Indonesia – it's not that the animals aren't there, but that we can't get to them.

I couldn't fully appreciate how awe-inspiring it was at the time, unfortunately. My stomach was aching, I was soaking wet yet constantly dehydrated, my muscles were cramping, my skin was literally rotting off, and I was sleeping less than four hours a night. After leaving, it would be over a week before I could wear shoes again as I needed to let my feet heal. Alex asked me at one point if I could appreciate the absolute beauty of the place despite everything, and I regret replying that I could not. But it was true. I was too sick and uncomfortable to see it. Even James, the perpetual optimist, lost his cool at one point and "just wanted to go home" – something I never heard him say before or since. In retrospect it was amazing, and I'm so grateful to have experienced all of it, but at the time – holy shit, I was losing my mind.

The sampan ride back and the subsequent hike up and down the volcano were about the same as the way there, except, like some cosmic joke, it stopped raining when we got halfway across the lake and didn't start in force again until we were back in town. After reaching civilization, one of our amazing guides, Sahar, invited us into his home for our first real family meal in weeks. It was one of my favorite moments of the trip. His family was there, taking pictures with us, and his kids were showing us their toys. Sahar's wife prepared a traditional Sumatran meal of rice, fish, veggies, and eggs. We also had some incredible local fruit called marquisa, which is an unusual variety of passion fruit with a hard shell that peels away to reveal little clusters of what look like frog eggs and taste citrusy. It apparently only grows at high altitudes in perpetually damp parts of the country like Alahan Panjang, where someone had picked it up for us. It was hands down the best fruit I have ever had in my life, and an incredible way to end such a tough trip. Sahar's home was so inviting and comfortable. It was rustic but felt warm, bright, and happy. Sitting in his living room was like hanging in a good friend's den. It just felt safe and good. The entire home was filled with the delicious smells of cooking, the sound of the pounding, unrelenting rain outside, and the laughter of his incredible children.

We stayed in a hotel in town for our last night. After the high that was Sahar's house, I almost forgot what every other moment in the country had been like. It quickly came back to me when I opened my bag and was greeted by quite possibly the worst smell I could have imagined. Everything was covered in mold. Everything. I took one outfit out, washed it in the shower with me, left it to dry in the hotel room (it didn't, but was at least only damp later), sealed that foul odor in my bag, and decided I'd deal with it back in Boston. After stewing on the plane and other transport for another few days, Anna described the bag as "smelling like wet death" when I finally did open it. That description seems appropriate.

We had our customary Cohiba cigar, provided by Barny, and local beer, provided by Jeremy, to mark the end of the shoot, and found out that we could sleep in the next morning as our flight wasn't until midday. Unfortunately, the elderly tai-chi society who met outside our hotel rooms did not get that message, because we all woke at 5am to incredibly loud EDM being blasted from enormous speakers, walked out of our rooms and saw a group of very old Indonesians exercising while James raved as if he had glowsticks and candy jewelry.

We were at the airport later that day, trying to find our

gate and wondering why gate 5 was between gates 11 and 32, when a worker told us: "The signs are meaningless, they are completely random. You must ignore them." I bought some absurd souvenirs, a case of kreteks, cracked a beer, looked for my friend Kim Jong-il and said goodbye to a country that had thoroughly confused and amazed me, and changed my perception of travel, for the better, for the rest of my life.

Chapter 3

The "Chick-in" That Wasn't

I'm not a picky eater. I am, in fact, a very adventurous eater, but I haven't always been. When Anna and I met, the most exotic food I had eaten was from a Chinese takeout place called Golden Temple run by white dudes with mullets. This was not because I wasn't interested in trying new foods, but because I grew up in a small town in Upstate New York where the front-page story of our newspaper was actually "Jacks has CHEESE!" the day the local burger place added the option of a slice of American cheese on your patty. With the first Pad Thai that Anna bought me (as a thank you for selling her my Chemistry books, notes, and old tests – yeah, I'm smooth), a culinary door opened that I have thrown wider than most. Her parents love cooking for me – a white guy who enjoys traditional Vietnamese foods. Jellyfish and abalone at a wedding? More spicy fish sauce please! Chicken feet and Heineken? I'd prefer a different beer, but sure. Duck fetus, blood-clot soup, mystery meat, tripe, cuttlefish – I love it all. The only item I continue to draw the line at is durian, the most disgusting food on Earth. Spending more than 10 years eating the delicious food at Anna's house opened my mind and made me not just prepared, but excited to see what different cultures could throw my way.

One of the most common questions I get when people ask about my travels is, "What's the weirdest thing you've ever eaten?" That's a hard one – what counts as weird? I don't say this to sound like a pretentious foodie asshole. I really don't even like the term "foodie", in fact, although saying that makes me sound even *more* pretentious. To me, foodie makes you sound like the type of person who uses phrases like "mouth feel" and Instagrams their scrambled eggs after putting scallions on them because "O.M.F.G. SCALLIONS! Best. Eggs. EVER!"

Tarantula is what's for dinner for one of the tribes I lived with and that's perfectly normal for them, but I obviously know that it's weird. In 2021 you can buy sushi in every grocery store in Nebraska, where the nearest ocean is over a thousand miles away and "foreign food" was unknown until the late nineties. But is it weird? Haggis is Scotland's national dish, and almost every pub there serves it. If you describe it (sheep's blood and innards mixed with some grains and cooked in its stomach), it sounds weird, and revolting, but no country is going to make their national dish something that tastes like shit, and it doesn't. In fact, it's delicious. Likewise for white and black pudding in England. Oh, and kippers! Kippers are amazing! Especially when prepared by Harry Marshall and served on freshly baked bread. England is not generally known for its cuisine, but I had a few of the best meals of my life there. The full English is the greatest breakfast in the world. What do we have in America? The lumberjack? The hungry man? Moons Over My Hammy? All magnificent, but they pale before the majesty that is the Full English. Black pudding, toast, tomatoes pan-fried in bacon fat, bubble and squeak, thick-cut bacon, sausage, scrambled eggs, fried mushrooms, and tea? Fantastic. (I know bubble and squeak is not traditionally part of the Full English, but it is for me.)

I think food culture in the US at least is getting over the idea of "weird". I see bone marrow and terrines on more and more menus, but when I described eating them on a trip to Paris in 2010, people were intrigued and slightly grossed out. With that said, I think there are still pretty well-accepted food taboos in 'Murica, and those are the ones I'll focus on, even those that make people a little sad when I talk about them.

Traditional Sumatran food is delicious – flavorful, delicate, perfectly balanced – but the food we had for the majority of the shoot was essentially "fast food". In general, everything was either loaded with sugar (even things you wouldn't expect to be, like eggs), covered in a strong brownish black sauce, very, very spicy, or just "off" in some way. Like delicious rice, eggs, and veggies, served wrapped in newspaper. Straight newspaper, the kind that leaves newsprint on your fingers, not some kitschy "Johnny Rockets" type wax paper made to look like newspaper. Nope, this was real *New York Post*-style newspaper – well, maybe not quite so biased, this was Sumatra after all. But either way, no one wants to grab a big bite of sticky rice with inky fingers only to uncover a story about a mudslide killing eight people as you plop it into your gaping maw.

We had some amazing meals prepared by friends of our fixers, and some unforgettable fruit. Most of it remains unidentified in my mind, but I can confidently recommend that if you're presented with any fruit from Sumatra, eat it! Well, *nearly* any. There is an incredibly popular fruit in Indonesia that is far and away the most disgusting food I have ever come across, as mentioned above. Everything about durian is terrible, and its cultivation could be used to disprove the existence of a loving god.

To start with, it actually kills people. Not from the disgusting taste or smell, which it has in abundance, but rather each fruit is like a natural flail. Imagine yourself walking on a hot, humid, sunny day when you see a tall tree – a *really* tall tree, with big broad leaves providing lots of shade. The ground under it is soft, cool, and inviting. You sit down, and there aren't even any roots sticking up to make this uncomfortable! At first you lean against the nice, smooth, cool trunk. This tree is a gift! Oh, someone must be looking out for you! You stop sweating, start feeling a little better, and decide that it's just too hot to go out there again. You'll just rest for an hour or so under this glorious, huge tree. You lay down on the cool grass, and all is right with the world. You shut your eyes, resting in complete peace. Then you hear a faint noise, a little "pop" and a "woosh", and think a bird must have just taken off. Then your head is crushed by seven pounds of spiky death that has fallen from about 160 feet up and reached a speed of approximately 70 mph before crushing your skull.

That's right, durian fruit is a seven-pound hobnailed projectile that falls from over 150 feet, impaling and crushing anything below it. God hates you. Let's say you jump out of the way in time. Maybe you opened your eyes to see the bird and – "HOLY SHIT WHAT IS THAT?!?!" Your peace and serenity gone, you inspect the harbinger of death embedded in the soft ground at your feet. Wondering if this could happen again, you pick it up and move away from the tree. Back in the baking sun, you start your investigation. You notice that this object looks diseased. It's an odd, warped, distorted-gastrula, and plain wrong shape, best described as Lovecraftian. (Don't you hate it when Lovecraft calls something "just wrong" or "indescribably terrible"? Oh, agreed that his overt racism is a much worse offense, but you're a writer, for Cthulhu's sake, describe something. Pick an adjective.) It's also covered in sharp spikes. Your hands are bleeding from carrying it, in fact. What is this terrible thing? Why am I being punished so? Angrily, you take out your machete (in my scenarios, you always have a machete – it's sweet and has dragons on it) and hack at the thing. Some ungodly terror oozes out – you can practically *see* the odor, it's so strong. Your senses are immediately assaulted – oh GOD, kill it! Kill it with fire! Your eyes and nose are burning! What is this terrible, terrible thing?

The exact smell of durian truly is hard to describe. Some say it's a mix of turpentine, onions, and the sweaty neckfolds of a dead and decaying obese pug. They aren't wrong. I would add an aroma of a back alley behind a Chinese restaurant on a hot summer night– that distinct smell of stagnant water, stale beer, and very rotten lo mein. It burns your eyes and nose like a chemical attack. It's banned from public transportation and most hotels in SE Asia.

A good friend of mine brought some durian to her grandmother, who loves the stuff. She lives in a nursing home in Massachusetts and was very excited to enjoy the delicacy, which she hadn't had in years. In the US you can only find frozen durian, which you generally leave at room temperature until it's thawed and smelling putrid. Her grandmother was so excited that she didn't want to wait for it to thaw, so put it on her radiator. After a half-hour visit my friend had to leave. About 30 minutes after that she received a phone call from the nursing home. Her grandmother was okay but they had to evacuate the entire home. There was an apparent gas leak and the fire department was currently investigating. A number of residents had irritated mucus membranes and most were complaining about a strong smell, but luckily everyone was fine. Her heart sank, and a few minutes later the phone call came, as she suspected it would: "What. Is. That STUFF in your grandmother's room?" The fire department had concluded their investigation – the source of the gas leak was an unknown substance on a resident's radiator, likely a chemical released from what appeared to be a melting... something. Durian. This is NOT the smell of anything you'd put in your mouth. I *love* stinky cheese – super stinky, moldy cheese. Some people may try to convince you this is how durian smells. They are lying. Cheese doesn't force a bunch of old people on respirators out of their beds and into the streets.

Okay, but how does it taste, you might ask. Fucking terrible, that's how. What possessed the first SE Asian man to put this in his mouth (not being sexist here but, guys, let's face it – you know it was a dude) is as great a mystery to me as how the recipe for Greenland shark came about (it involves the use of sheep urine, multiple fermentation cycles, and burying the meat underground for months to detoxify the flesh). An even greater question is – once they had eaten it, why did they do it again? Nothing about it screams "edible".

The consistency is a combination of hard and slimy, like biting into a tumorous tendon in undercooked chicken. It wriggles and slides and releases juices, but is firm and distinctly creamy. It's meaty, like a cashew fruit, but feels rotten somehow, like a very overripe avocado. The taste is truly horrific. It is overpoweringly strong, like a mouthful of hot garbage. The closest description is a mix of rotten onions and raw garlic with an edge of very cheap vodka.

Alfred Russel Wallace, a personal hero of mine whom we named our son after and is the coauthor of the theory of speciation by means of natural selection (I bet you thought it was all Darwin! The story is long and complicated, and Darwin absolutely deserves all of the attention he gets, but Wallace had a pretty sweet beard also), loved durian. This fact alone makes me question my admiration of the man (along with his advocacy of spiritualism and being a forerunner to the 21st centuries anti-vax campaigning but only briefly. He was an amazing biologist and early environmentalist, and clearly deserves more recognition than he gets. So, here he is in this book for his love of the most disgusting food on Earth. Sorry, Alfred. He quotes others when he says, "its flavor surpasses all other fruits in the world", but, in his own words (with my own thrown in because I'm an ass), "its consistence and flavour are indescribable [pig excrement comes close]. A rich custard highly flavoured with almonds [what almonds did they have in the 1860s? Could Wallace have been given rotten onions rolled in the rotting carcass of a skunk and told that they were almonds?] gives the best general idea of it, but there are occasional wafts of flavour that call to mind cream-cheese... Then there is a rich glutinous smoothness in the pulp which nothing else possesses [besides rotting meat and the insides of maggots], but which adds to its delicacy. It is neither acid nor sweet nor juicy; yet it wants neither of these qualities, for it is in itself perfect [*cough* bullshit *cough*]."

I've been told that durian is used to punish misbehaving

children in SE Asia. They are not forced to eat it, which would be cruel and unusual, but are instructed to kneel on its sharp and evil exoskeleton in the corner. As terrible as this sounds, I think a Dickensian punishment for children is the only logical use for it.

Inexplicably, some people besides Wallace *love* it. Many people, in fact. My mother-in-law is one of them. Every time she visits, she fills our house with its overpowering aroma and laments the fact that she can't get it at all in Hawaii (where she lives), and only frozen in Boston (where we live). "The frozen stuff just tastes so weak," she says, as I gag and leave to wash my eyes. She insisted I only hated it as much as I did because I'd never had it fresh, so when I saw a man with a durian cart outside of the zoo in Sumatra, I stupidly asked the crew if we could have a snack break.

Our guides immediately warned me that durian is not for the faint of heart, like I was some amateur. This wasn't my first rodeo, boys – I've eaten things that would make a weaker man beg for relief. I've had my share of frozen durian, durian cookies, durian pastries – all my mother-in-law's failed attempts to win me over to the durian-loving population. Fresh durian? Sure, why not? I'm here, when in Rome and all that. The familiar odor greeted me – oh it *is* much stronger fresh. Wow, didn't think that was possible. Okay, I can get past that. Texture – if anything worse when it's fresh. Slimier, more rotten – oh God, why did I do this? And the taste – yes, yes it is *much* more complex when it's fresh, and that is absolutely not a good thing. Holy shit. My mouth, my nose, my eyes were on fire. The guides were laughing, I needed anything to kill this taste – Pocari Sweat to the rescue.

After my ill-advised durian excursion, we filmed all day at the zoo, enjoying a wonderful lunch of McDonald's takeout. The next meal we had was at a little café where Jeremy, our guide and fixer, assured us the food was "not disgusting." To start, we had lots of shrimp chips – think pork rinds, but shrimp instead of pork fat. They aren't bad. You eat them because you're hungry, they're in front of you, and they're salty and crunchy, but I wouldn't seek them out. Anna would. She says it's a nostalgia thing. She grew up eating them at karaoke parties, and once in a while really craves them. She equates it to my love of circus peanuts. If you eat them for the first time as an adult you'll probably think they're disgusting, but I have memories of elderly friends of the family giving them to us kids as a special treat. Okay, I get it – shrimp chips as a starter.

We bought beers from a little shop down the street and ordered a round of juices for the table (six of us). Then we ordered nine main courses – mostly egg and noodle omelets, a few rice-based plates, and some seafood, with four side dishes consisting of various fried delectables. The food was, as promised, not disgusting. In fact, it was pretty good. It was served on plates, with chopsticks, and with no newsprint in sight. It wasn't overly sweet, and the sauces seemed to enhance the flavors of the food rather than smother them à la TGI Fridays. We were all enjoying this! We didn't even need the beer to kill the flavor – in fact, the beer was delicious with the fried sides. We ate everything, but that was because we were six guys who hadn't eaten in eight hours, had been out in the sun most of the day, and are all gluttons. There was a lot of food. And the bill? $25 US, total! Jeremy told us we were not getting the local price and he could argue the bill if we wanted. Absolutely no need. This was more than worth $25.

We liked the place so much that we decided to go back the next day. We had spent a long day filming and planned on another obscenely large meal, but we had grown arrogant and forgotten where we were, as well as our unfamiliarity with the language, customs, and cuisine. We thought, based on the previous night's experience, that we could order anything on the menu. This was a good place, with nice waiters, good food, and available beers, right? We would be brought down by our own hubris.

I am a huge proponent of the "please bring me anything that's good" move in restaurants. It has rarely failed me. It drives a few of my friends crazy, and they look at it as further evidence of my inability to make a decision. Truth is, I can make decisions, but only do so when I care about the outcome, which is rare. I love food, all food. If the wait staff or chef in a restaurant thinks something is good, I probably will also. I started doing this when I started going to places where I couldn't speak the language or read the menu. It wasn't too hard to motion "anything that costs this much" while holding up some local currency. It afforded me the opportunity to try a lot of stuff that I probably wouldn't have otherwise, and although I didn't know what any of that stuff was called, the vast majority of it was delicious. You too can benefit from this slightly adventurous risk with great success if you follow these rules:

1 Make sure you are not allergic to anything. Any possible food allergies kills this as a viable option, as some viable food options may kill you.

2 You must truly be open to any food. If you're the type of person who says, "I like all music," but when I look at your iPhone I see only top 40s and nineties hip-hop, this is not a realistic move for you. Know yourself and own your shit. There is nothing wrong with 90s hip-hop.

3 You can't be secretly hoping that the waiter/chef will choose the fish tacos. Wait staff and chefs are nice people, but are not mind readers. If you want fish tacos, order fish tacos.

4 Don't add a lot of qualifiers, it doesn't make you adventurous, it makes you annoying. "I'll take anything – but nothing spicy, no pork, nothing too rich, and nothing fried please."

5   It has to be a good restaurant – this move does not work at any restaurant where the wait staff does not like you or the food they are serving you, or they are forced to wear or say something which they would not normally wear or say. Examples include – suspenders, black-and-white checked shirts, or a greeting like, "Welcome to *blank*, would you like to try our new *blank* smothered in *blank* and fried your way?"

In Sumatra, we were good on the first four, but clearly didn't think through number five. *Was* this a good restaurant? It certainly wasn't a *terrible* restaurant, right? I realize now, the only good things said about it were, "It isn't disgusting," and "We got a shit-ton of food for $25." A good restaurant this does not make. In fact, it brings to mind one of my favorite quotes from the series *Veep* – "Any restaurant that serves anything by the fuckload is not a nice restaurant."

Well, Jeremy wasn't with us, nor were any of the other guides, we'd had enough of ramen-noodle omelets and decided to live dangerously. "Five of anything, a few other things, and some drinks. Like last night, please," we proceeded, arrogantly. Alex went and got the beers and also picked up an iced mocha drink about which, after glancing at the ingredients (cocoa, palm oil, sugar, and coffee), James exclaimed, "Wow, that's basically deforestation in a can – let's skip these from here on out." We dug into shrimp-puffs, not a bad start. We moved onto some fried things. Yummmm, fried-y. Next came out rice and... meat?

It clearly was meat, but none of us could guess what kind. It was coated in something, pan-fried, and the animal had been cut in pieces but served with no head, which was unusual for a small animal. Was it rat? I had eaten rat before and was okay with it. It seemed to not be the right shape for rat, though. We asked the waiter, "Excuse me, sir, what is this delicious-looking meat?"

His response, in very stunted English, was, "Chick-in." Huh. Okay, not the answer I was expecting, but clearly good enough for James, who dug it, and said, "It's pretty good. *DEFINITELY* not chicken though." There were some drumsticks which *might* have been chicken, and probably were, but I've never been served chicken ribs before. It would have been very rude to not eat it, so I had some. The ribs tasted like very dry, very gamey pork, as did some unidentifiable body-parts that were almost McNugget shaped. The waiter stood by while we ate. "Delicious, thank you. Chicken, yes?" I said, pointing at the mystery meat. He smiled back: "Yes, good, chick-in." Okay, let's go with that. Everyone but James appeared a little uneasy, despite all telling the waiter that it was "great" and thanking him. He was still hanging out, watching us eat, smiling genteelly. We ate some more fried stuff, had some more rice and veggies, added some various tabletop sauce options to things, and avoided looking at the ribcages on our plates.

The waiter then tapped me on the shoulder and pointed outside as a small animal ran past the door. He smiled as things started to click in my head. Realization dawning, I nervously asked: "Chicken?"

"Ah, yes. okay," he said with a smile. "Yes, yum."

No, not yum. Conversation had stopped as the words sunk in. James stared in wide-eyed horror, and the rest of us chuckled a little to ourselves. "So, I think we've figured out the rib situation. Mystery solved." A couple more chick-ins ran by, playfully chasing each other and mewing while they pounced on roaches in the electric glow of the restaurant's neon sign.

Chapter 4

A Little "Me" Time

"Hey, Pat, Pat, Pat, yeah you alright? Morning! Yeah, it's still raining. Um, so, I had an idea that today's the day for the tree! *Exciting* huh?"

That was Barny's way of waking me up one morning and letting me know it was going to be another wonderful day in Sumatra. A day where I'd finally get to answer the question no one had asked, "What's it like to spend an undetermined amount of time alone in a tree in the rainforest?"

Barny, like everyone at Icon, is absurdly well-traveled and the type of person you just want to be around. I describe Barny as the cool older brother everyone wishes they had. He has some of the best stories you've ever heard and the personality to tell them. While never loud or obnoxious, he has a commanding presence that immediately draws people to him and makes you not only trust him, but want to please him. This is the perfect personality for a great producer. I trusted every decision he made, no matter how crazy it seemed, and genuinely wanted to be a better presenter because of him. Barny gave me invaluable direction and tips without ever getting frustrated with my inexperience. He also has a degree in biology and looks like a blue-eyed male model. He always seems to have just come from somewhere fascinating and is quickly on his way to another amazing place with gorgeous people and interesting food. He has an effortless "cool" about him that seems to radiate, and his slightly harried air only adds to the mystery that is Barny's life outside of the time you are with him. He's typically seen with mussed sandy-brown hair, a button-down shirt covering a muscular upper body, and stylish jeans. I continually questioned why I was on one side of the camera and he was on the other. The only reason I could come up with was that I was an American – and Americans like to watch other Americans.

Barny also had a lot of ideas for episode "acts" – distinct parts of the roughly 42 minutes per episode of screen-time that make nice, succinct, digestible scenes to keep an audience engaged and watching in between commercials while driving the story forward towards some reveal at the end. Some of these would "end" (cut to commercial) with a cliffhanger – usually me seeing something on a camera trap whose images I'm looking through, jumping off of something, or hearing something that I can't immediately identify. The "reveal" on these comes right after the return from commercial – "Oh, Pat jumped awkwardly and stumbled, how embarrassing" (true story), "Turns out that lizard I thought I saw was really a cow at weird angle" (true story), "That's a picture of a dude in tiny bikini briefs – not a dinosaur" (true story). Others contained a mini-story in and of themselves that had a start, middle, and a resolution, where whatever I learned would then be a launching point for a new phase of the investigation, would turn the episode in a new direction as the lead I'd followed had turned out to be a dud, or, I'd learn a bit of information that I could bring back up at the end summation.

Barny is a master of crafting these Acts. He taught me that it's one thing to tell people a fact, but another to demonstrate it. It's easy to say, "The Baka are excellent hunters and trackers and can read the forest as easily as we read a book. It's very unlikely that they're actually seeing a rhino when they say they are seeing Mokele M'bembe" (a supposed living dinosaur). People get it, that makes sense. This tribe needs to hunt to survive, they know rhinos, okay, point made – keep going. Barny, though, could make this point an act. He would put me in a loincloth, hand me an elephant spear, and send me out into the forest with a group of hunters from a pygmy tribe and then I could *see*, along with the audience, that they were not going to mistake one animal for another. It was way more engaging that way. Sure, it led to ant stings, dehydration, parasitic infections, and a bee landing on my exposed penis (true story!), but, that point definitely got made for the camera and it kept people watching. Butts. In. Seats.

A lot of these side-adventures ended up on the cutting room floor – like the Pinkie Incident – but the tree plan felt like a winner. Barny's idea was, "Let's show people how hard it is to get a photo of an animal in a rainforest." This is true – it is remarkably hard. People see magazines like *National Geographic* or documentaries like the *Planet Earth* series and think that you just stumble across these animals while hiking. The truth is, the stills/scenes that are shot purely in the wild take weeks or sometimes months to capture, and are shot by a professional photographer, targeting a single species after additional months of research and consultations with guides and experts on said species in said location. Just your average person out walking with a smartphone is very unlikely to get a good picture of any animal in true old-growth, off-the-beaten-path forest, much less an animal that is rarely seen where we have no definitive idea of its habits, patterns, or even its waking schedule – is it nocturnal? Crepuscular? Etc.

To show this, Barny said, in a pre-shoot crew meeting back in Bristol that Anna happened to be at, "Yeah, I thought we'd stick Pat up in a tree for a bit. Maybe a day or two. Alone with a couple of cameras. He can record himself and see what animals he might find," and everyone sort of smiled and nodded. Anna said, "That's nice. You'll get a little 'me' time I guess, Pat," and everyone laughed, except for me who was finding out that I'd be alone in a tree for a couple days in the middle of a rainforest.

Well the day was here. I wasn't nervous about being alone for a day or two – I'm good with alone time. I've spent countless hours alone in labs and field stations all over the United States. I don't really get bored and I can daydream like a champ and let the hours just melt away. My concern was that, left completely to my own devices – I get a little stupid and complacent. This is also why I've never held a gun. I'm convinced I would forget I had it in my hand after holding it for a bit and, while gesticulating, shoot myself or someone else. I could see me using the gun like the detectives in *Plan 9 from Outer Space* – finger on the trigger, scratching my head with the barrel and telling people, "You make a good point," while motioning at their terrified faces with the gun. I've accidentally cut myself many times from unconsciously scratching an itch while holding a knife or other sharp object.

I lived alone in a barn for a marine bio internship when I was 16. I didn't have anything to do one Saturday, so, I decided to go into the lab and pick through a three-year-old sample of estuarine seaweed looking for larval fish, amphipods, and copepods under a dissecting microscope – as 16-year-olds do with their spare time. This was part of an ongoing research project at the facility, but, they had gotten really backed up on the work of "fish picking" as it was called because it was tedious, time consuming, really stinky, and no one wanted to do it. I didn't mind any of those things and was excited to be contributing to the depth of scientific knowledge in some small way. One key thing that was stressed in my "fish picking" instructions was that these samples were stored in formalin – a really noxious solution of formaldehyde that's used to preserve scientific samples – and therefore could only be opened and sorted through in a fume hood, which would suck-away the toxic fumes.

That Saturday morning, I went into the lab, found my sample, brought it to the scope in the fume hood, broke out my forceps, probe, and petri dish, and started picking. Holy shit it smelled bad! Formalin is really nasty stuff. I only noticed the smell for the first 30 minutes or so, then I got really into the work and was excited by what I was finding. A couple hours later I realized that I'd forgotten to eat that day, again, and my eyes must have been starting to get a little tired because the sample was blurring. I stood up to stretch, and immediately passed out. Just for a few seconds. I came to, lying on the floor of the lab, and realized that while I had the sample in the hood, I had neglected to turn the hood on, so the room was full of formalin fumes. I couldn't really stand up, so I crawled out of the lab and into the fresh air. I started feeling better after a few minutes and was able to stand up, get some lunch, and finish the sample by dinnertime. Which was a bag of baby carrots and some peanut butter because I'd also forgotten to go grocery shopping.

So what I was worried about with Barny's tree idea was how much damage I could do to myself in the time I was left in the tree. Everyone laughed when I voiced this, but Anna spoke up saying, "He's not joking. He's walked into traffic multiple times, regularly knocks over children, and will probably drop the camera, if he even remembers to turn it on. There are a lot of distracting things in the rainforest right? Lots of bugs and plants on the tree he'll be in, lots of interesting sounds and butterflies? Yeah, you'll either get a ton of random weird footage that he's shooting at some crazy angle, or, he'll fall asleep and fall out of the tree."

"He'd fall asleep? Knowing there are tigers, Sumatran rhinos, tons of venomous snakes, sun bears, and gibbons nearby?" asked Barny, as if I wasn't in the room.

"Oh, for sure he'd fall asleep. [Turning to me.] None of those freak you out or even make you nervous right?"

I shook my head.

"Yeah, none of those animals worry me. He knows what he's doing with animals. The main thing that can hurt Pat, is Pat. He needs a job at all times, something with clear guidance that he needs to accomplish, otherwise, he'll be asleep or hurting himself."

She wasn't wrong. In my mid-twenties I was filming a "talent reel" with a ton of dangerous reptiles. Giant constrictors, rattlesnakes, a forest cobra, huge monitor lizards, alligators, crocodiles – you get the gist. I spent an entire day playing with them, handling them, feeding them, posing with them, etc. – then ended the day driving myself to the hospital with a massive head wound. Not from the animals, but because during a break from filming I'd tripped over my own feet and split my head open on one of their cages. It required two staples and while I was receiving a lecture from one doctor for driving myself to the hospital with a head wound, another asked if some students could watch the process as they had never seen head staples before. I said sure. A half dozen very young looking med students then walked in and started asking me questions about animals, filming, and my injuries while the doctor shaved and prepped the area. When the first staple went in and one of the students said, "WOW! That shit is CRAZY!" and another said, "I think I'm gonna puke" – I asked what school they were from. They turned out to not be med students as I'd assumed, but sophomores in high school visiting the hospital on a fieldtrip.

So, in Sumatra, like the Griswolds before us, we set out into the forest looking for the perfect tree. Instead of snow and freezing temperature though, we had oppressive heat and pouring rain. Shouting to be heard over the incessant rain as we walked, Barny ran through the plan with me one more time.

"So, on Anna's advice, we're going to keep you busy up there. Keep your eyes and your ears open for any animals and try to take any still images or video shots that you can of them. You'll also do a piece to camera every 15 minutes. James has packed you extra batteries that should last two days, but, we won't leave you up there that long. You have food, water, and a walkie but…"

"I know, 'don't use the walkie unless it's an emergency'."

"That's right – we want you to be isolated, we want you to get into the feel of the forest up there. That's also why I'm not telling you how long you'll be alone there."

Barny didn't know this, but I knew Healthy and Safety at Icon hadn't cleared a night alone in the tree, so I was sure I'd be coming down by dark at the latest.

"I think this looks like a good spot. Yeah – I noticed this tree on one of our hikes the other day, remember? And, worst case, you know this area because we've been here a few times on walks – one of our camera traps isn't too far – so, you could make it back to camp on your own if it came to that right?"

"100% no. I have absolutely no idea where we are and would definitely wander off and die if I tried that."

"Oh, mate, you can't be serious? You don't remember that spot we just passed? You did a piece to camera after catching a cool lizard," James piped up.

"Nope, that was at night, and if I had to guess I would have said that spot you're talking about is down the other trail – the one where you have to go through all of the stinging nettles. We went through the thorns to get here, not the nettles, right? I definitely got torn up by thorns."

"Yeah, mate, that's a different patch of nettles you're talking about – the big patch of nettles and the swamp where Barny lost a shoe are right back that way. The mud just isn't as deep today."

"Listen to yourselves and think about me walking back to camp by myself. Honestly, guys, I'm not worried about this. I won't wander off, I'll chill in a tree, watch some cool bugs, hopefully see some cool animals, maybe get some footage of a sun bear! That would be amazing, and we know there's one around here based on those tracks we found. Don't worry, I've got this."

Alex spoke up, "Yeah, we'll be back for you. Just sit tight until then. Need a boost? I think we're at your tree!"

And we were. It was certainly a big tree, in a pretty spot, like nearly all of the trees we had seen. Everyone believed this to be the one "we" had scouted, and it had stopped raining! Simon climbed up first, making it look very easy, and declared that there was a good nook for me about 12 feet up. I tried to follow him and fell on my ass. After we were all done laughing, Alex lifted me up to a good spot where I could get some better grips and climb up to Simon's nook. I got situated, took the cameras out and found perches for them, tested them, got my snacks out, and took in my surroundings.

It was the first time that we were in the middle of the forest, away from camp, and it wasn't a downpour. It was shockingly beautiful. The dappled light was streaming through trees that were well over 150 feet tall, making a gorgeous canopy, but there was also dense underbrush – trees and shrubs of all sizes, and everything was covered in epiphytes, mosses and vines. I was sitting on a branch facing the trunk with my pack in front of me, but could easily turn in any direction to see whatever there was to see.

I said goodbye to the guys while they filmed, and then started my first piece to camera – with the lens cap on. James noticed and told me I might want to do that one again. As soon as their voices faded and the sounds of insects and birds picked up, it felt more remote. The more still I was, the louder it was. I started seeing birds that a few minutes before I had only heard. I tried taking some pictures of them, then getting some video, but with no luck, so I just watched them and marveled at the life all around me. I watched the bugs on my tree and wondered how many of them even had a scientific name – so many insects in Indonesia have never been classified. Oh shit, I missed my first 15 minute check-in. OK, piece to camera number two.

I had some snacks, sang some songs to myself, had some water, watched the bugs, saw more birds, saw another tree shrew (still no pictures – the experiment worked!), missed another 15 minute interval, and then the first hour was up.

I spent most of the next hour watching ants. I almost fell out of the tree following one that was really interesting looking – she was bigger than the rest and I was wondering if she was actually an ant mimic when I started to lose my balance, but I didn't fall. I did miss another piece to camera, though – I had to pay more attention. I left the lens cap on while filming a bird, and then did another piece to camera about leaving the lens cap on. This was very enjoyable, but not going great from a "content" perspective.

In the third hour I was really getting the rhythm of the forest. I was singing and humming along with the birds and bugs, then I heard a troop of gibbons and I remembered to film myself hearing them – with the lens cap off! I followed their progress in a huge loop all around my tree in the tree tops, then lower, then back up, but I couldn't see one, I could just hear them making these wide circles for about 30 minutes. They knew I was there and were actively avoiding coming within sight of me. It was amazing.

In the fourth hour, I saw a lot more birds – one even landed close by me and I missed the shot by a split second. I ate more snacks and drank more water, I sang more. Then I realized I had to pee and, because I was facing the trunk, I didn't want to pee directly forward or it would likely come back and I'd be sitting in a puddle of my own urine, so I decided it was best to roll off the side and precariously hang half my body off the branch. It worked, sort of. At least I wasn't sitting in a puddle and I hadn't fallen off the tree – even if it was super awkward and unnecessarily complicated and dangerous.

Towards the end of the 4th hour I heard a loud noise in the underbrush and got really excited. I turned the camera on and started whispering about how there was a huge animal moving maybe 50 feet from my tree. Then I took the lens cap off and did it again. I couldn't see the animal, but it was loud, and definitely getting closer. Forty feet and it was louder, and making weird noises. Could it be a tapir? They are primarily nocturnal and spend most of their time in water. A rhino? A tiger? A sun bear? That prospect suddenly seemed more scary than exciting. Thirty feet. Yes, it has to be a sun bear – what else is that big out here? I could see dense foliage moving and rustling – something that stands maybe three or four feet tall was moving through it, directly towards me, slowly, grunting and making very odd guttural noises. Holy shit. Was this an Orang Pendek? Was I about to see OP? Was OP about to attack me?

This 100% did cross my mind, and I considered it a very real possibility – it was as likely as a sun bear in that moment. Ten feet away. Then it screamed, a primal, terrifying, heart-racing scream, and I screamed and grabbed my knife and pointed it at... Simon, in a ghillie suit with full camo makeup, covered in mud, and laughing hysterically 12 feet below me.

Then the other guys came out from behind some trees about 50 feet away, also laughing, and reminding me that it was all on camera and my mic was on, so, my singing, running monologue about the beauty of the forest, etc. – all on tape. They had been there for about 45 minutes, watching me and recording me on a long lens – out of sight, while Simon changed into his gear. After my awkward peeing, they decided it was time to send in Simon and he started belly-crawling his way to me.

"What *was* that, mate? Why didn't you just stand up, have a wee, then get back into your spot?"

This was a logical question, and my answer was it didn't occur to me to stand up. I was supposed to sit in the tree until they came back, and standing didn't seem like an option.

They were dumbstruck, but impressed that I had managed to not fall. They did impressions of my scream and knife fumbling for the rest of the trip. I hadn't managed to actually expose the blade, so at worst I would have thrown a heavy Leatherman at OP or a bear. My heart was still racing but I had to admit it was a really good prank. And I had really enjoyed my "me" time in the tree. It was one of the few relaxing moments I'd had since we arrived in Sumatra.

When I asked Barny if he thought it would work for an act, he replied, "Well, maybe a ½ depending on your footage. Did you remember to turn the cameras on, take the lens cap off, all of that?"

"Um, most of the time," I admitted – Barny shook his head. We had some really great moments for the outtakes reel – but nothing that made it into the final episode. Anna was just impressed that I didn't fall out of the tree, cut myself, or fall asleep. This is a pretty big win in a situation where I am alone in a jungle.

Chapter 5

Orang Pendek – "The Little Hairy Man in Sumatra...

... No, Not the Man Selling Fruit. Smaller. Yes, the One That Lives in the Forest. Not the Weird Old Man in the Hut; the Animal-thing that Steals Sugar. With the Big Penis, Yes."

Hello there, and thank you for making it this far with me. We've come to the "cryptid", or mysterious animals that may or may not exist, chapter of the book. This is either a very weird turn in the funny travel book you've been enjoying, or you were *very* confused by the first few chapters of the cryptozoology book you purchased. I will not be citing my sources here (most of them are my own notes and memories anyway). Feel free to Google anything I mention and write angry e-mails and nasty tweets about how I got the total number of islands in Indonesia wrong. This is not a paper in a scientific journal, it's a collection of true stories from my personal experiences and some of my opinions. When making *Beast Hunter* we needed to cite at least two credited (peer-reviewed or expert-opinion) sources for every fact I stated on camera. There was a factchecker at Nat Geo whose job was to pick apart every line that was said. Most networks do not require this, but it's one of the reasons I love Nat Geo so much, and why Nat Geo is among the most respected brands in the world. This did, however, mean that our job of making films about animals that may or may not exist was very difficult. There were so many retakes in order to throw in a "perhaps" or a "some experts say" that we ended up doing a five-minute reel of me just repeating phrases that imply ambiguity in different intonations which we could cut in during editing. In reality we loved the scrutiny, and I feel it made the series much better than your run-of-the-mill crypto show filled with statements like "that's definitely a werewolf" when someone hears a barred owl; or an episode with more night-vision footage than a wannabe actor's "break-out" video (regardless of whether the proposed animal is nocturnal or not) and lots of loud noises and Blair Witch-style nausea-inducing camera movements followed by, "What's *THAT?!?*", or – in my opinion, the biggest crime in this field – faked news stories or actors playing scientists. That is bullshit, I say!

There were a few things in *Beast Hunter* that were cut by our factchecker which I would still argue were true. We had to cut a whole segment when I caught a hagfish because I said, "They aren't closely related to anything else, and they really aren't even a fish by a strict definition." I may have *slightly* overstated how different they are evolutionarily, but I maintain that what I said was true. My friend Zeb, a real marine biologist, is probably cringing reading this. But it's that kind of scrutiny and adherence to the truth that I think set our show apart. Anyway, there is no factchecker on this book, other than you, dear reader. So, check away – but, as I said, these are mostly my own thoughts, opinions, and experiences.

In case you haven't figured it out yet, I am a nerd. Not like, "I'm going to dress like Harley Quinn for Halloween," but like, a real nerd. Specifically, a science nerd. This differs from the so-hot-right-now comic-book/sci-fi nerd. Sure, I liked *Fringe* as much as the next guy, I've read all of the *Song of Ice and Fire* books to date, and my high-school friends and I stayed in on Friday nights to watch *X-Files*, but my true nerd status really becomes apparent whenever a conversation strays into any topic in biology.

I advocated for the name "Darwin" if our first child was a boy, and when we found out we were having a daughter I tried to convince Anna it would still make a great middle name. We ended up naming her Luna after the amazingly beautiful and mysterious *Actias luna*, the luna moth. Yes, I'm aware that Luna Lovegood is a character in one of my favorite book series – she's one of Anna's and my favorite characters, in fact, but that's an added bonus for the name rather than a driving force. Our son is named Wallace Charles after Alfred Russel Wallace, Charles Darwin, and Charles Fort.

I was a teaching assistant for multiple chemistry and biology labs and audited extra biology and philosophy classes – for fun. I traveled to Maryland to observe horseshoe crabs mating – again, for fun. One of the only real fights I can remember getting into with my best friend since birth was when we were eight and he insisted that crabs were amphibians. The only TV shows I watched in the eighties and nineties were nature programs. Whenever I was sick and off school I was allowed to rent anything I wanted from the video store. My pick was always a volume of *Life on Earth*. David Attenborough, Alfred Russel Wallace, and Charles Darwin were my childhood heroes, and remain my adult heroes – in addition to Harry Marshall, the founder and head of Icon Films and the man responsible for sending me on all of these adventures and forever changing the course of my life. He also makes damn fine TV.

When I left home at 16 and lived on my own for the first time it was for a marine biology internship in Maine. A friend asked what the nightlife was like in southern Maine. I replied, with no hesitation or sense of irony, "Great! It's really awesome! There are foxes, raccoons, lightning bugs, polyphemus moths, and so far I've spotted two species of owls!" I also read the *Fortean Times* and *CryptoZooNews*, and most of the people I follow on social media are naturalists. Don't worry, though – I won't get *too* scientific in this chapter (and there will be poop jokes).

I say all of this because, in recent years, there has been a move towards hijacking nerd culture by moderately cool people. An actor who can't quite cut it turns to fantasy shows and suddenly he's a heartthrob. A few years back, even Charlie Sheen "led a search for the Loch Ness Monster". I happened to be in Scotland investigating the same monster at the same time he was, and heard some horror stories from the locals about his behavior in their beautiful country. I am not a person who does this stuff for the attention – I do it because I love it, am fascinated by it, and think it doesn't do science any favors to simply write off the things that sound bizarre.

Too many scientists forget that the general public does not consist primarily of other scientists, and that most people would rather hear about the *possibility* of a bipedal intelligent ape walking around the Great North Woods than the reality of the new barnacle you discovered. Run with that – talk about the *possibility*. It will get people listening. Then throw in some stuff about wolverines, the reintroduction of wolves, and pine martens. Make them things that people, real people, will find interesting. Throw in some jokes, give some sexy facts. More people would have been interested in your lame barnacle if you led with the fact that it has the largest penis-to-body ratio of any animal in the world. It's over six times the total length of its body! That's CRAZY! And fascinating! And memorable. Where do they keep it? How do ... I'm getting sidetracked; the point is — don't refuse to talk about something because you think it sounds silly.

Getting people outside for a homemade Bigfoot expedition still gets them outside, and they *will* see other amazing and exciting things, even if they don't see a sasquatch. A generation of Bigfoot hunters might turn into conservationists, or field biologists, or maybe lawyers who want to protect the land they loved exploring as a kid. Another interesting side effect of not immediately writing these things off, all of you closed-minded scientists out there, is that sometimes, *sometimes*, you might find that there is actually *something* to these stories. If you go out there, use your scientific training, open your mind, dispel disbelief and really look at the facts and evidence, you might surprise yourself, like I did with Orang Pendek (OP from here on out) and others.

With all of that said, I'm an open-minded skeptic at heart, and I approached everything around *Beast Hunter* as such. There is a famous quote regarding Occam's razor that goes something like, "When you hear hoofbeats in the distance, you don't think it's a herd of unicorns. You think of horses, and you're probably correct." I also think of horses, but am willing to be shown the evidence for unicorns. I did have a "mistaken identity" theory for each cryptid in the series; however, I was more interested in the cultural significance of each myth than its veracity.

The story of OP is incredible – the habitat loss, the legends, *Homo floresiensis* being discovered on a neighboring island, the bizarre biologic diversity of Indonesia (tiny elephants and giant lizards), the seemingly contradictory theories of Island Gigantism and Island Dwarfism on display in the same location, and introducing people to a culture and a world that are quickly disappearing. It all made me so excited to investigate this myth. In my mind, though, it likely was a myth – mistaken identity for an orangutan or gibbon, or possibly stories passed down from a time when humans and hobbits (*Homo floresiensis* have been affectionately named hobbits after Tolkien's little furry-footed humanoids) lived together some 10,000 years ago, which isn't really that far back.

I don't want to say my mind was made up when I arrived in Indonesia, but I was about 80% convinced this was mistaken identity. There were a few things nagging at me, though, a few little details that made me really excited to explore this legend for myself. One of the biggest was Jeremy Holden's sighting.

I'd followed Jeremy's research for years and had a huge amount of respect for the guy. He's identified a bunch of new species, has had at least one named after him, and has taken some of the most difficult-to-get photos in the world – mostly in Sumatra – including the only photo ever of a Sumatran rabbit. When Jeremy publicly states that he believes in and has seen OP, it certainly makes you pause before you write it off. He is so well-respected that Flora and Fauna International funded a 15-year research project led by Debbie Martyr (an accomplished tiger researcher) and Jeremy to document OP. Nat Geo also funded a five-year photo project that Jeremy was involved in. I won't reopen old wounds and fuel the fires of controversy, but from the outside, it had sounded to me like these projects were sunk more by infighting, bureaucracy, government interference, local conditions, and just bad luck than any lack of evidence.

There have been a bunch of other eyewitnesses over the years, but eyewitnesses are notoriously unreliable. Your brain makes weird associations with things that you only catch a glimpse of. It's been shown how difficult it is to judge size and distance on water or in open fields, and people tend to see whatever they are looking for – most "Bigfoot" photos are a Rorschach test of blurred branches and shrubs. The crypto community has even coined a term for these images – Blobsquatches.

I try to find witnesses who are not looking for anything in return – ones who are even a little hesitant or embarrassed to tell their story. My favorites are the ones who have already questioned themselves dozens of times and ruled out every other possibility. Ideally, they saw the animal under good conditions, in full view, for a few seconds at least, when they weren't looking for it. Jeremy Holden met all of my criteria for a great eyewitness and exceeded my expectations because of his knowledge of local wildlife. The best witnesses meet the above criteria and have some background in biology or other wildlife fields – scientist, photographer, hunter, fisherman, game warden, etc. One of my favorite biologists is a man named Mutt Merritt, who runs an oyster hatchery associated with the University of Maryland in the United States. I worked for him one summer and he taught me a lot about fieldwork. One of his best pieces of advice was that, if I really wanted to find out about the local wildlife, don't talk to scientists, talk to the people who are in the animals' environment everyday – the fishermen, the hunters, etc. Most scientists go on "field expeditions" for short stretches of time while the fishermen are on the water every day, observing. They know breeding habits, behaviors, migration patterns, the movements of food sources, the effects of climate, and a lot more, even though they may not know the Latin name for the animals you're asking about. Geographically-isolated groups of animals behave very differently to other populations, and the locals can tell you about local animals. A textbook (or Wikipedia, whom I am quoting here) may say the following regarding the diet of Siamang gibbons (*Symphalangus syndactylus*):

> *The siamang eats mainly plants. The Sumatran siamang is more frugivorous than its Malayan relative, with fruit making up to 60% of its diet. The siamang eats at least 160 species of plants, from vines to woody plants. Its major food is figs (Ficus spp.). The siamang prefers to eat ripe rather than unripe fruit, and young rather than old leaves. It eats flowers and a few animals, mostly insects. When the siamang eats large flowers, it eats only the corollae (petals), but it will eat all parts of smaller flowers. When it eats big and hard seeds or seeds with sharp edges, it will peel out the fruit flesh and throw away the seed.*

All well and good – there's a lot of useful information in there. If you're a scientist reading this description, you'll notice the telltale signs for when siamangs are about – look for figs, unripe fruit and older leaves left alone while ripe fruit and young leaves are eaten; look for flowers with only the petals eaten and piles of large seeds discarded. Great, that helps. But, if you talk to a local hunter they'll be able to tell you all of this, and, in the next breath, say, "But lately they've been eating mostly grasshoppers because we've recently had an explosion in their numbers." Or they'll be able to tell you which trees are flowering or fruiting right now, or maybe, "This time of year they usually have babies, so they aren't foraging as high in the mountains as usual," etc. You get my point. This was the basis and main premise of *Beast Hunter* – talk to the locals, they know their shit.

When Harry Marshall was searching for the Yeti in Bhutan (he has, no exaggeration, the best stories of any person I have ever met – his house is like an endlessly fascinating museum filled with items he's collected over the years), he came across a local guide who told him outright that the Yeti was real – he didn't know what it was necessarily, but he knew it was not mistaken identity for a known species. When Harry pushed him, he described its ecology – when it ventures into the high mountains, when it returns to the valley, what it eats at different points in the year, etc. Harry asked how the man could know this and he replied that he knew it the same way he knew what yaks ate, or when the local bears were mating. Finally, he said, "You Westerners are crazy. None of you believe in any animal until a white man has given it a funny name."

Incidentally, this same guy led Harry to a spot where he collected hair of "unknown origin". He had a DNA analysis run on it and the results showed "no known match" at the time. In 2013, it was finally matched with a polar bear species in an area where no polar bear has ever been known to live. Harry found DNA evidence that they are still alive, and likely the source of the Yeti legends. Why a movie has not been made about this man I will never understand.

In Sumatra there are, as is usual when it comes to cryptids, massive variations in the eyewitness testimonies. Some describe OP as furry, with fur color varying from black to red to yellow, others as hairless; some as tall (up to 5 feet), others as very small (maxing out at 3 feet); some as ape-like, some very human. Many people in the scientific community point to this as "proof" that the animal is a myth. I think that's being a little glib, personally. Look at the variation between regional populations of orangutans, for instance. From one region to the next they vary in size, color, and behavior. Add in sexual dimorphism and age, and you could wind up thinking you have two or three distinct species. This is the path that many cryptozoologists have gone down for OP. Adam Davies and Richard Freeman, two well-known OP researchers, have been to Sumatra a number of times and used some of the same guides we did. They've concluded that there are two distinct species: Orang Pendek being more pongoid (great ape, bigger, furry, etc.) (hominid), and Orang Kardil being more human-like, similar to *Homo floresiensis* (hominin). I've never spoken with Adam, but I hear he's a nice guy, and my correspondence with Richard has been very positive. I'd recommend each of their books for anyone looking to do further reading on OP.

Loren Coleman has broken OP down into even more potential species. I've known Loren fairly well for years and respect his opinions on many cryptids. I consider his *Field Guide to Bigfoot and Other Mystery Primates* as required reading for anyone interested in the subject. These researchers and others who feel the same may very well be right – at some point in time there may have been multiple species of hominin in Sumatra, but I'm going to refer to any unknown nonhuman primate in the region as OP for the purposes of this book. Also, since the media likes to misinterpret things like this, it should go without saying that when I refer to OP or any other cryptid in this book I am referring to a *species*, not an individual animal. I don't believe there are any true researchers or crytozoologists who actually think Bigfoot is one individual creature who has survived for hundreds, maybe thousands, of years, and yet some news outlets continue to word their articles in this way just to poke fun at the very notion that the animal could exist. This tactic really only shows their own ignorance, closed-mindedness, and lazy reporting. There are a hundred different ways to refute the existence of Bigfoot, so why resort to lying? I'll also say that just because I enjoy reading a lot of different crypto books doesn't mean I believe them all. I look at them as theories that we can seek to prove or disprove. Loren's books are a cut above the rest in my opinion – excellent, engaging reads and they show his scientific background.

Corroborating the eyewitness accounts were odd footprints which looked like a cross between a person and an orangutan (without getting technical, it's all about the position of the big toe), but footprints are also "fuzzy" evidence – they're easy to fake and, in a place like a rainforest, are often naturally distorted by weather and substrate. Even a well-cast footprint can be misleading – there is the classic bear-that-looks-like-a-human print, and there are sun bears in Sumatra, but there are other things capable of making weird prints in a jungle, including one animal walking on another species' tracks, and simply the terrain. It's rare to find a "trail" of tracks on the forest floor – usually it's one or two in a muddy spot before giving way to leaf litter again. One or two tracks can barely even be called "tracks" because of the multitude of possible distortions.

Harder evidence came by way of hair samples that didn't appear to be a known species but were too damaged to have DNA extracted (allegedly, there is some DNA analysis showing an unknown nonhuman primate, but this isn't accepted by most scholars, who say the results are inconclusive at best), and there were some blobsquatch photos. The most compelling evidence to me, before arriving in Sumatra, consisted of the credible eyewitness sightings, and the indisputable fact that a species of small hominins lived on a neighboring island in fairly recent times.

We heard about some great sightings and I'll detail a few of my favorites. I'll start with a quote from one of our guides, who asked that his name not be recorded but did share his own sighting with me. He described OP as golden blonde, with a muscular body too thick to climb trees gracefully (I would dispute this as I've seen a silverback gorilla gracefully and effortlessly climb a 40 foot tree in seconds, and you don't get more thick and muscular than a 500 pound silverback), very comfortable on two legs and "walking like a ghost" – meaning with arms in front of it, outstretched. This exact description came up a lot, and when I started questioning him about it, clearly implying it might have been a gibbon, he stopped me and said something which made me pause and have my own "white people give it a funny name" moment. He said: "The people who don't believe in Orang Pendek are people who don't go into my forest." Essentially, he was asking, "Who are you to tell me what I did or didn't see?" and implying, "Would it be different if I had a degree or spoke your language?" Touché.

Sahar Dimus

Sahar was one of the most respected and prolific OP guides and is the creator of one of my favorite pieces of memoribilia from the series — a hand-drawn image of the OP he saw. It's framed in my office, and looking at it reminds me daily of being out in the field with him. Sahar knew the forest of Kerinci Seblat National Park as well as any living man and could tell you anything you wanted to know about the animals that lived in it. He had always firmly believed in OP, despite not seeing it for himself until 2009. His parents and grandparents spoke about OP the same way they talked about gibbons, orangutans, tigers, and rhinos. It was a known, real, identified animal, although rarely seen. There was nothing supernatural about it – no legends, or myths. In fact, there was more of a spiritual connection with tigers (who many in Sumatra believe to be both spirits and real animals) than with OP.

To illustrate this, Sahar suggested we speak with a shaman

who performed a ritual to summon the spirit of the tiger to protect us as we ventured into the forest. The shaman told us that, while tigers were both spirits and real animals at the same time, OP was more mundane. It seemed that everyone thought it was odd that it walked upright, but attached no special meaning to this. Sahar and our other guides (as well as a surprising number of folks who lived on the edges of the forest) told us that OP was more common when their grandparents were young, but it was always rare, and now they weren't sure if there were any left. They didn't say this in a way that raised suspicion, like, "I really do have a model for a girlfriend, but she lives in Canada and doesn't have a phone," they said it matter-of-factly. They said the same about rhinos, tigers, and some bird species. The sad truth is that extinction has become a fact of life in Sumatra, with palm oil plantations, slash-and-burn agriculture, and urban sprawl taking over what was once lush contiguous rainforest. In their minds, OP was just another possible casualty of modernity. Sahar and others were hopeful there were still a few around, but not convinced.

Sahar brought me to the exact location where he saw an OP the year before. He showed me the places on a line of small saplings that an OP grabbed as it ran away. There was an unmistakable mark on each tree in a location consistent with an animal about three and a half feet tall, with long strides, a long reach, and that was running with its arms outstretched and grabbing the trees as it passed. These marks appeared as damage to the moss covering these trees, and it looked consistent with a human-like hand grabbing and sliding down slightly, as if pulling the tree a little while running by. I tested this on similar-sized trees and produced nearly the same mark. It was evident that it wasn't fresh (no one did it while we were there), but was still distinct, so about a year earlier seemed right. Could Sahar have faked this? Sure, but I didn't get the sense that he did or would. It seemed like, if he was going to fake evidence for us, it would have been much bigger than this. A footprint is easy to fake and we would have loved it. A hair sample can be faked or planted. This was impressive enough to be exciting, but unimpressive enough to be real.

He said he saw the animal crouched on a stump, holding a branch for support, either looking out at something or maybe eating grubs. Sahar wanted to get some physical evidence, but the animal heard or smelled him and bolted. He didn't see its face, but he saw it jump down, land on two feet "like a man would", and run, also on two feet. He said it was very fast, and didn't seem to be exerting itself. It moved with very graceful strides, arms in front, grabbing the trees as it went. This motion was similar to a sighting described to Richard Freeman by a farmer, Pak En. I asked Sahar to mimic the motion, and he did, in very fluid movements. He described the fur as coarse and tannish colored. He said its musculature was evident – it had strong shoulders, broader than a gibbon's.

The way it moved and the coloring reminded me of a gibbon, but Sahar said a gibbon would have climbed or swung to get away, and never have jumped to the ground when the threat was there. He also said the proportions were off – OP had high and broad shoulders, and shorter arms. He did say that it was most similar to a heavier, more muscular gibbon. Not at all like an orangutan.

Sahar's sighting does seem like it was probably a gibbon, on the surface. Could an oddly proportioned gibbon make the decision to make an exit on foot rather than going up a tree? Sure, even though I never observed this behavior, especially when the threat was on the ground. Every gibbon I've encountered has retreated by going up a nearby tree as soon as the opportunity presents itself. I'll admit red flags were going off in my mind when I read over the writeup of his account. I misidentify snakes all of the time. I think I've found a milk snake, and then look closer and after a few seconds realize it's a young black racer. I've mixed up ring-necks and red-bellies, garters and ribbons, etc. Does this mean I'm a bad field biologist? No, it means animals show variation and often a glance isn't enough to provide a positive ID, even for the most seasoned fieldworkers. I'm thinking, "Gibbon! A gibbon might do that! That sounds like a gibbon's build! Pat, you said on international TV that you believed a man saw an OP when clearly it was gibbon!", but that's me sitting on my comfortable couch, with my wife next to me, in our comfortable home. When I was in the forest with Sahar and he was pointing out signs of animals that I never would have noticed, or describing in great detail the habits of every imaginable creature – from walking sticks to fruit bats – I would have never been so arrogant as to question what he told me he saw, so why would I now?

Well, I wouldn't. But I do have to remind myself of that. The facts are the easy part – it's the interpretation of the facts that takes decades of experience to get right. Could a gibbon have behaved this way? Sure. Is it likely? No, not at all. Can my pug run around the house three times? Absolutely. Has he ever done it, or will he ever do it? Definitely not. Sahar knew the forest as well as I know my dog. He knows gibbons and knows their behaviors and movements, to the extent that he could predict where a gibbon was going to go before it went there. While we were in the forest he spotted some gibbons and described the exact path they would take, and he was right. Could he mistake a gibbon for a different animal the way I mistake species of snakes? Sure, he's only human. But is it likely? It absolutely is not.

There are nearly no consequences if a field biologist makes a slight error like those snake examples above – we'll generally figure it out before anything bad happens. We won't mix up a venomous and nonvenomous snake though, ever. Why? Because there *are* consequences. I will never mistake a timber rattlesnake for a hognose, but I might mistake a hognose for a rattlesnake for a second, but definitely not the other way because there are consequences, and we know that subconsciously. The consequences for Sahar making any mistake in Kerinci Seblat – any mistake, any misidentification, such as reading the weather, the depth of the river, or the slipperiness of a muddy hill wrong – is death. Could Sahar have mistaken a gibbon for an OP? Yes. Did he? No, I don't believe he did.

Did he lie to me? No, I don't think he would do that. For those skeptics who didn't know Sahar and won't take my word for it – if you were a guide who made a sizeable portion of your living bringing people into the forest to look for OP, wouldn't you lie about your sighting earlier in your career, if you were going to at all? Rather than 15 years after you started looking and had already been established as a "go-to" guide for many expeditions. If you did decide to lie, wouldn't it be a more detailed sighting, at least seeing the animal's face? No, I think Sahar was finally able to see the animal that he worked for so many years to bring into the light in the land he worked to preserve, and he deserved to. More than most people.

Zairudin

Zairudin did not have a last name, which confused my American mind at first. In Indonesia, however, Mononyms are not just for rock stars and divas; they are actually fairly common. Even a couple of former presidents rock the Bono/Cher vibe. Speaking of names, in researching OP, I've found that "Pak" is disproportionately the name of many eyewitnesses compared to the total populace. I found a Pak En, Pak Jintan, Pak Nadur, Pak Mega Harianato, Pak Entis, Pak Suri, and, yes, even a Pak Man. But I digress.

Zairudin (Z from here on out) and his family were farmers on the edge of the forest on the outskirts of the village of Pondok Pisang. He had been a farmer for many years and knew all of the stories about OP, but had never seen one himself. His parents and grandparents used to tell him about them, and also that their numbers had dwindled to the point where they weren't sure if he would ever see one. There was no sentimentality in this, it was just stated as a fact. As I said before, the people in Sumatra treated disappearing species as part of life. Z did, however, have an affinity for the local tiger. He loved knowing it was out there, and took great joy in seeing it some early mornings or evenings. He said that a few "Chinese businessmen" offered him the equivalent of five years' salary to kill the tiger and give it to them. He refused, saying that if he killed the tiger it wouldn't keep the population of pigs in check, and soon they would eat all of his crops. I really liked him for this. It was this kind of future planning that was far too often not in the realm of possibilities for many of the people we met, who were sadly just trying to survive today. It was disturbing to hear the prices for illegal wildlife, however, and you could definitely see the draw of poaching for many young people in the towns who didn't see too many other options for themselves ever to make that kind of money.

Z was just a likeable guy all around. He was very short and thin, but hard – an incredibly muscular man. His entire body was taut. Despite having a name that sounded like a bad guy in an *Expendables* movie, he had a smile that brightened his lined face, which he displayed often. He was balding and looked to be in his early sixties, although I was told a few different ages for him, putting him somewhere between 38 and 55. He looked a bit like an Asian Patrick Stewart, and James and Alex would say "engage" in their best Jean-Luc Picard voice anytime Z's name was mentioned for years after.

Z had seen OP twice. Once at a distance, where he wasn't completely convinced, saying, "It kind of looked like a gibbon, kind of like an orangutan, but people told me it was an OP." The second time he saw it he was much closer. The animal broke into his hut while he was sleeping, and this is the sighting we wanted to document for *Beast Hunter*.

It is obviously startling to be woken up by animal noises coming from a few feet away when you live in an area where tiger sightings are not uncommon. Z's family was gone, visiting in the nearest village. He said he often spends weeks alone on his farm, his family splitting their time between the city and their farming outpost. He was glad his family wasn't there, and said his first thought was of gratitude that they weren't in any danger. I thought this was really touching. His next thought was that maybe they had unexpectedly come back in the middle of the night, and he was worried that something was wrong. He sat up in bed and saw a "hairy man-like animal" standing a few feet away eating sugar from a bag he kept in a woven pouch tied to the ceiling to stop mice and rats from getting to it. It hung at about belly-button height for me, which would be chest height for Z, and a little below eyelevel for the animal he saw.

The animal didn't appear to be afraid at all and was enjoying the sugar, reaching its human-like fingers into the bag and eating pinches of it. Z didn't register what it was and watched it for a little while. He thought it was a "monkey" (gibbon), until it turned around and they made eye contact. He described it as very strong looking, very broad and wide, like a bodybuilder. When I showed him a hair-color chart he pointed to a golden sandy blonde and said it was pretty close to the color, even though he said it was "black". (An interesting side note here – nearly all Indonesians' natural hair color is black. When describing anything as "hair", remote villagers always call the color "black"; if they said "fur" they would describe a spectrum of shades. I brought a L'Oréal hair-color chart with me which a lot of viewers thought was really funny, but it helped overcome this language barrier. A witness might say "black" but then point to a blonde or an auburn shade on the chart.)

Z said the hair covered most of its body but its face, hands, and feet were hairless. He also described hairless sexual traits. He said it was about three feet tall (just under one meter) and stood very confidently. When trying to describe its face he kept saying "like a human monkey". When I asked him what he meant he said it was flatter than a gibbon's face. From the back it looked very much like a broad, strong gibbon, but the face was much more human. I showed him pictures of different primates. He had never seen a gorilla before, but said that its nose was similar, but not quite the same. I got the impression that there was no bridge to the nose – not quite as absent as with the skull-faced macaque (first photographed by Jeremy about a year after I met him), but not as prominent as on most apes. Z described the eyes as "human", eerily so – intelligent, unafraid, and thoughtful.

He said that after making eye contact he jumped up in his bed and grabbed his spear (which he sleeps next to). He pointed it threateningly at the animal, saying he wouldn't have actually killed it because it looked too "special" – too human-like – but he didn't want it in his hut. It vocalized little, low, "ooghf, ow" guttural exhale noises, bass-like, and then grabbed the board it had ripped off to enter the hut, stooped, and exited.

Jeremy and I asked some clarifying questions, rephrased what Z had said to see if he would change details about the encounter (he didn't), added details of our own to see if he would correct us (he did), and both felt that he was credible and telling the truth. Jeremy decided to ask for more details about the animal itself. Z did get a good look at it, after all. His description was a familiar one – a human-like ape, apparently intelligent, and seemingly very powerful but not aggressive. It didn't seem to be too afraid of Z, but wasn't exactly crawling into bed with him either, like a domestic dog. (Get that erotic fan fiction out of your head. Amazingly, there is a huge market for erotic cryptid novels. Author and mother of two Virginia Wade reportedly made $30,000 a month for a few years self-publishing works in this genre. She would have been pleased with where our line of questioning went next.)

Jeremy then asked if Z had seen the animal's genitals. At first, Z seemed surprised, and then smiled. No one had asked him that before! His wife started laughing – clearly, she had heard about this, even if no one else had. Yes, in fact – he *had* seen its genitals, and he was impressed! It had a "very strong penis". He said it wasn't *too* long (his wife slapped him and blushed at this), but it was wide. He said it was very prominent and the girth was impressive. Flaccid, it was as wide as a broom handle and maybe 2-3 inches long. He measured with his fingers and his wife blushed again and started laughing.

This is extremely unusual among primates. Humans are alone amongst the great apes with their prominent penises. Most ape penises are very small and thin, to the point of being difficult to identify as male when flacid. OP's member sounded much more human than ape. Jeremy had heard this description before, which was what prompted him to ask.

It was clear that Z didn't have an agenda. He had seen something odd and was happy to talk to us about it, and that was all. There was no status that came with this sighting, no legions of folks lined up to hear his story. He wasn't bragging about his bravado for facing down the bloodthirsty beast – he saw an OP, it ate some of his sugar, he scared it, and it went away. Period. No more supernatural than pigs trying to eat his crops, and less impressive than the local tiger, in fact. He seemed amused that we even wanted to talk about it. He was more interested in showing off his farm and hearing our stories about different places we'd been and animals we'd seen. OP is part of the native fauna – he was happy it was still around, but nonplused in general. It was a great sighting – this was a man with no stake in the story, who was knowledgeable about local wildlife, and who saw the animal's face (and penis) up close, in decent lighting (candles and a bright moon). That's about as good as you can hope for.

A few months after we interviewed Z a couple of researchers

from Holland published an interview with someone name Pak Man. The details of his sighting were nearly identical to that of Z with a few specifics changed – Pak Man didn't see any genitals (I'm so happy I could write that sentence); the animal was eating sugarcane as opposed to granulated sugar; Pak Man grabbed a spear as the animal was walking away, whereas Z grabbed a spear to scare the animal away; in Z's story the animal broke a board to enter his hut, in Pak Man's it broke a board to leave. It almost seemed like a story in a game of "telephone". The fact that Pak Man didn't mention anything about genitals combined with Z's reaction to our question about them ("You're the first to ask!") leads me to think it *may* have been a case of Pak Man wanting some limelight.

I've seen this before. In West Africa while filming an episode about a living dinosaur, we came across a couple instances where people hear a story and adopt it as their own, believing it will get them some attention or maybe even money. Without questioning Pak Man myself I can't say that his story isn't just remarkably similar to Z's. They live in similar conditions, both being farmers on the edge of the forest, and maybe OP looks at these farming outposts as a good source of food, and both farmers could conceivably sleep with candles burning and spears nearby (despite having numerous guns for hunting birds). I honestly can't say, but I think the more expeditions to Sumatra looking for witnesses and the more word spreads that Westerners are looking to interview – and maybe even pay – local people who have seen OP, the more likely we are to get false accounts.

Jeremy Holden

I've already introduced Jeremy and his sighting was covered in great detail in the episode of *Beast Hunter*, but I'll highlight it here as well. Jeremy came to Sumatra in 1994 looking for adventure and animals to photograph. He heard the legends of OP and, in his own words, "thought it sounded like a bunch of bollocks". He was a seasoned traveler by the time he arrived there, and planned on spending a bit of time taking some pictures before moving on. While Jeremy does not have a degree in biology, he is one of the most knowledgeable field biologists I have ever met. He's like a walking encyclopedia of the flora and fauna of Sumatra, with the combined knowledge of a trained researcher and a local hunter mixed with the incredibly detail-oriented eye of a professional photographer. I suspect he may have a nearly photographic memory as well. His mastery of languages is remarkable. He's also introverted, humble, incredibly respectful, hotheaded when he feels something is unjust, and very funny. He gets frustrated at himself when he can't think of the Latin names for various insects (the name almost invariably comes to him minutes later), and identifies reptiles like an experienced herpetologist, saying things like, "No, no, it's not a *trianguligerus*. It's clearly a *pelias*. Just look at the gastrosteges and the subcaudals."

He was interested in getting some photos of tapirs and was on a potato farm on the edge of the forest one late afternoon when he found some strange footprints which looked like a mix of orangutan and human. He followed them and started noticing signs of foraging. Some roots had been dug up and apparently eaten, some torn banana palm, some ginger with the stalks twisted in a way that showed immense strength – the animal seemed to be sampling small amounts of a lot of different things rather than binging on one item, as most animals will when presented with an abundant, available food source. Most animals find some tasty roots and they eat as many as they can. Who cares that there is ginger nearby? This animal seemed, in Jeremy's words, to "use the forest like a supermarket buffet" – very human-like. He followed the tracks to the edge of the forest where he noticed swaying palms a little ahead of him. He cautiously walked forward and saw birds mobbing an animal, as if it had disrupted their nest (he thinks it may have taken eggs). They were divebombing it and it was making annoyed "Mau-Mau" sounds. He froze – what he saw was an upright walking animal, but seemingly more human than ape. Its back was to him, but he sensed it had realized he was following as it started off in a different direction. He stood transfixed, unable to move, forgetting to even lift his camera to his eye.

He described the OP as "built like a wrestler or American Footballer", or alternately "like a brick shithouse". He did not see its face but said the head rested on the shoulders, with no real neck to speak of. He said it was bigger than a gibbon but shorter than a man, and golden tan colored. What struck him was the way it moved. He said it wasn't hunched or on tiptoe, but "walked like a supermodel" with complete fluidity. He said this was not an animal that occasionally walked on two legs, but an upright walking nonhuman. He said it was emotionally overwhelming to see it. He started crying because he had such a visceral reaction to seeing something so similar to us and yet "other" – separate. It was bizarre to see an "animal" that moved like a "human" – it's a method of locomotion that is unique to humans and one of the things that separates "us" from "them". He was so moved by the sighting that he dedicated more than 10 years of his life to spotting it again and getting a photo – something he has not managed to do. He feels he was close to it a couple other times, but the brief glances he got were not enough for his scientific mind to definitively say it was an OP.

I absolutely believe Jeremy, and not for the reasons you may think. One reason was his complete certainty in what he saw. This was a man who questions everything – he second guesses, looks at things from every angle, and takes all possible evidence into account before making a decision. He is also more than willing to change his mind if compelling evidence is put forward. He told me he's thought about that sighting almost daily since it occurred, has replayed it in his mind, questioning every aspect of it, looking at every other possibility, and has ruled out everything other than "this was an unknown primate". Also, Jeremy is a man who does what he wants when he wants to do it. He doesn't take root in one place because he likes being mobile. He is fiercely independent, rarely taking a job that requires more than a couple months commitment. To say he doesn't like to be tied down is an understatement equivalent to saying, "Sumatra is rainy." Also, Jeremy, to put it mildly, does not love living in Sumatra. He hates the weather, the food, the language, the constant bureaucratic battles that are required to do anything, the inability to get the government to make any changes, the daily struggles to accomplish any task, the isolation – everything. He made some amazing friends that he really cherishes, Sahar being one, but said most people never accepted him and always treated him like an outsider. He went to a market nearly every day for 10 years, and said every single day people tried to rip him off and take advantage of him. The only reason he stayed as long as he did was because he knew OP was real, and he wanted to be the one to get a picture of it. This, more than anything else, made me believe him. If he had any doubts about what he saw there is no way he would have stayed as long as he did.

Dr. Mike Morwood

Like so many aspects of *Beast Hunter*, my interview with Mike was a longshot that none of us expected to work out, but which, against all odds, did. Ben, the producer of the Canada and Brazil episodes, had a great quote about filming: "We get to find someone somewhere in the world doing something *amazing*, ring them up and say, 'Hello, yeah, we want to join you and do what you do for a few days', and they almost always say 'yes'. It's the best job in the world!" Mike, amazingly, said yes. Mike was not a cryptozoologist, although he is a god-like figure to most of us. Dr. Michael J. Morwood was one of the top anthropological archeologists in the world. He was a published author and an innovative archeologist bringing entirely new techniques to the field. He was best known to the world as the discoverer of a new species of human, *Homo floresiensis*. Luckily for us, Mike was also one of the rare scientists who sees how important the public is in advancing his area of study. Mike wanted the general populace to care about archaeology and recognized that multimedia outlets could help with this, even a show named *Beast Hunter*.

I met Mike on my way out of Indonesia. We had an eight hour layover in Java and everything that day had gone wrong, as was to be expected. Our initial flight was delayed, and our good friend and Java fixer Uncle Jimmy was back, and he got the pickup times wrong. He brought a "special" car for us, into which we could not fit both us and our gear. He acted shocked, despite having carted us around for three days when we first arrived, and knowing full well how many of us there were and how much gear we had. We waited at the airport while he tracked down another car and Alex attempted to contact Mike.

No one could get a hold of him, or anyone he worked with. It appeared that the dates had been confused on Mike's team's end. There was a conference in Europe where his entire team was presenting information about *H. floresiensis* (for ease of writing [my own laziness] I will just say "the hobbit" from here on out). The plan had been for me to meet Mike in his lab and view the most complete hobbit skeleton he had uncovered – the one he'd used to name the species based on it – as we spoke. We finally reached some folks who said the skeleton was not there – it was with the researchers, while others said it was in a different lab in Sumatra, others a different hobbit skeleton was there which people had not seen yet, and others just bone fragments were at the lab. Another phone call informed us that someone from the Indonesian government had misplaced part of the skeleton, another that we would be filming with a life-size replica, and yet another that the lab was entirely locked-down and no was allowed in. The phone calls were fast and furious, with Alex getting more and more confused and upset. Barny, to his immense credit, was taking it all in his stride, saying he knew it would work out one way or another.

After a couple hours of multiple phones going and numerous stories, it seemed we would not be able to film in the lab as no one in Java had a key, or possibly the government was confiscating all of the skeletons while the team was in Europe. We could, however, meet with Mike, who amazingly was still in town. We arrived at Mike's hotel, a bit jostled after another exciting Javan car ride. Unfortunately, Mike was not feeling well, and was unsure if he would be able to meet with us. We completely understood and resigned ourselves to make the episode without him or the hobbit skeleton.

As we were on our way to lunch in the lobby of a nearby hotel, Mike called saying he'd taken some medicine and was feeling a bit better. He was interested in talking if we were. We absolutely were. Mike met us in the lobby of his hotel and did not seem as vivacious as in the interviews I had seen him in. He said he must have picked up a bug somewhere, and he and I shared "sick in Indonesia stories". Oddly, it later turned out neither of us had picked up a bug, but in fact we both were starting to feel the first symptoms of cancer. Mike's would unfortunately take his life a year or so later. Mine, stage 3, was operable, but would change my life forever.

We walked to an outdoor café down a side street where Mike said we could get away from the traffic noise for an interview, which would have to be brief as we needed to be at the airport in a couple hours. We set up, whereupon all of the equipment began to fail – lights, cameras, sound recorders, mics, all of it. It had been punished, as we had, with two weeks of near-constant torrential rain, and had had enough. James, in his role as the

MacGyver of the team, started rigging things with duct tape and cable ties while Mike and I sat and had a fruit juice. He thanked me for letting him tell his story. I was shocked – one of the top archeologists in the world was thanking me, the host of a cryptozoology show. I told him it was an honor to meet with him and promised that *Beast Hunter* wasn't the typical crypto-show, and that we looked at things from a biological and anthropological angle.

"It's on National Geographic, right? That's all the assurance I need," he said, before talking about certain things which I have always felt and have already expressed in this book – that is, the world needs some mystery, scientists need to know how to talk to people and get them excited, and so on. He also said the hobbit finding had changed his mind about a lot of things. He invited me to Flores, the dig site, to see that they were still finding bones of hobbits. He also told me that, in Indonesia, it was easier to get a film crew into places than a scientific expedition, so I should check out the far side of Flores where he had reliable reports of lizards larger than Komodos, but where no herpetologists had been allowed to document them.

By this point, James, superman, had rigged something usable, and we were ready to film. I had avoided the topic of the hobbit and its possible connection to OP while Mike and I chatted, but now jumped right in. Mike's answers left me speechless. He thought that the hobbits survived on Flores until the 1920s. He said there were credible accounts of them being there when the first Dutch settlers arrived on the islands. He also said he had some physical evidence of this, but wasn't ready to publish it. I was floored. Another species of humans interacting with modern people – not "modern people" as in *Homo sapiens*, modern people as in "people my grandfather's age". He went on to link stories of Ebu Gogo, a mythical race of cannibalistic humans, to the hobbits and maybe OP, saying they might be distorted stories of the same thing. Ebu Gogo was typically described as an old woman, but Mike said it could also just be very short people. There is a legend of the last Ebu Gogo being killed shortly after Westerners arrived – it was tracked back to its cave and locals beat/stoned it and its family to death. Mike thinks this could be the true story of the killing of the last, or nearly the last, of the hobbits on Flores. He thinks the cannibal part was a myth caused by fear of an animal far too similar to us for comfort, and likely less sophisticated.

I asked him if he thought the hobbits could still be on one of the remote islands in Indonesia and, without pause, Mike, in his amazing Australian accent, said, "What are there, over 17,000 islands in Indonesia, and less than 1,000 of them are inhabited? Yeah, I don't see why not. I think it's fairly likely, in fact." My jaw dropped. Here was one of the most respected scientists in the world saying that there could be a surviving race of hominins on an Indonesian island. It was earth-shattering for me. Despite the difficulties of the last three weeks, the pain, the skin rot, the leeches, etc., I wanted to go back out there, right then. How could I not? Mike Morwood said he had evidence that hobbits had lived alongside people up until the 1920s, and it was "fairly likely" they were still living on some of the more remote, isolated islands. Fantastic. With our jerry-rigged equipment, we only caught pieces of our conversation, but it was enough to give us a great segment and for me to confidently say I was a believer.

We shook hands, thanked Mike, and rushed back to the car wishing him well. As we were leaving the café owner appeared. He could not have been more than four and a half feet tall. He walked over and said, "You found me!" in a squeaky voice. We all looked at each other, confused. He said, "I heard you talking. You are looking for Orang Pendek. You found me!", and started laughing hysterically. He asked if he could take a picture with the giant, and Alex obliged. It's one of my favorite pictures from the trip – this tiny man, beaming, with his arms wrapped around Alex's waist, hugging him tight. The man then showed us his car – a hot pink 1970s Pontiac with "Thug Life" decaled on the dashboard. God I love Indonesia.

My thoughts on OP

Jeremy believes that OP is more man than animal, a hominin – a relative of people closer to us than a great ape. The other eyewitnesses I spoke with are not sure – they think it could be an ape or a man, and are actually not too concerned with the distinction. Some consider orangutans to be people (I found a similar mentality in West Africa regarding chimps and gorillas). I believe that, if OP is still around, it is likely a large, primarily ground-dwelling close relative of the gibbon. I also think there may be another species, more human-like, related to the hobbits of Flores, but the reports I heard and the things I saw led me to believe that what people have been reporting in Kerinci Seblat and other locations in Sumatra are a remnant population of an unknown great ape closely related to a gibbon. I do not have any hard evidence of this, and I did not think this before I investigated it on location. I do believe that they were there up until very recently, and there may still be a few, but I don't think it's a species that can survive.

Sumatra does have large swathes of rainforest, but most of it is broken up into plots, divided by highways, expanding towns, villages, farms, and palm-oil plantations. There is not that much contiguous forest left. As the human population grows, so do the resource needs. Farmers keep expanding, a few acres at a time, up mountains. Rubber and palm-oil monoculture is replacing old-growth forest at an alarming rate. The known primates in the area are having a hard time coping, much less a species which, in the guides' own words, was "always rare". Our guides said that, unlike gibbons and orangutans, OP is a "wanderer" – never staying in one place, without a real "home range". A species like this is not unheard of (the arctic fox, for example, has an apparently endless range), but it does require vast amounts of continuous habitat, which OP would no longer have. Kerinci Seblat is vast, unexplored, and very difficult to access – perhaps this is why most reports in recent times come from areas on its outskirts. Maybe it holds the last few Orang Pendeks – aging, and confused by what they see on the edges of their land. Maybe they are trying to make use of the "new" land – eating crops as Jeremy observed, or breaking into huts like Z's and Pak Man's. Z had said something that stayed with me – in his grandparents' stories, they occasionally saw little OPs, presumably young ones, but his parents didn't. Most of the great apes don't occur in large numbers naturally, and a wandering one would likely have even smaller numbers (like whales). They would also probably be long lived, so it's possible that Jeremy and Z saw one of the last ones – an elder, a survivor, who adapted to the new life provided. But adaptation is different to evolution, and it seems like it might be too late for the species.

I'll continue to speculate, based on what I know and what I think I know. People ask:

Why haven't we found a body?

That's an easy one – visit Sumatra and tell me how many bodies you find in the forest, of anything – tigers, tapirs, rhinos, orangutans, birds, lizards. Even a spare bone here or there. You won't find any. In a rainforest, bodies are gone within days and even bones decompose, are buried in some event like an earthquake or rockfall, or eaten quickly. Caves provide one of the only places to find bones, and that's where the hobbit skeleton came from. Mike said that if scientists keep exploring the cave systems in Indonesia using similar techniques to his, he was confident that more incredible discoveries would be uncovered. I wholeheartedly agree.

Why don't we have a picture of one?

Here's an experiment for you (I actually did this in Sumatra) – go to a rainforest, climb a tree, stay up there for a few hours alone, have your camera out and ready, and see how many clear, focused pictures you get of animals. I didn't get any – a few blobsquatches, but not one good picture. I saw a bunch of stuff – but just for a few seconds. That was with no rain (miraculously, it was the only three hours of that excursion with no rain), my camera was out and ready, and I was sitting still. Very few people ever venture deep into the rainforest in Sumatra, and for good reason. Those that do don't often have cameras out and ready, and are not stationary – even if you stand still you are picking leeches off yourself, swatting mosquitos, and doing other things that make noise and alert any animal to your presence. I had a troop of gibbons howling all around me when I was in that tree. I thought I was being silent, but they knew I was there. I heard them make a huge loop all around me, but didn't see a single one. What about camera traps, you say? Jeremy Holden is, debatably, the best camera-trap photographer in the world. He says, "If an animal doesn't use trails, we have virtually no chance of getting it on camera using the technology we had in 2007." Every animal he has ever photographed was on a trail.

Jeremy theorizes that OP doesn't use trails, and there is some evidence to back him up. To the best of my knowledge, OP is usually sighted "off trail", when someone is wandering in the forest. Unlike other animals, it isn't reported on trails when it's spotted or when it runs away from people. Game trails would also be the likely place to find footprints, but, to the best of my knowledge, most alleged OP footprints are off-trail.

OP might also be nocturnal, making it still more difficult to get a photo of. Most sightings occur at dawn, dusk, or night. There are no nocturnal apes, gibbons being the closest (sometimes active at night). If OP was crepuscular or fully nocturnal, it would be even less likely that we would see one. Its behavior of breaking into houses at night seems to lend some credence to this, if the eyewitnesses are to be believed.

What about tigers?

A school of thought goes – if there was a ground-dwelling nonhuman primate, tigers would eat it. This is simplifying it a bit, but it's the basic argument. I would say that a tiger may occasionally eat an OP, a young one probably, but I don't think it would wipe them out. Jeremy thinks that's why OP is so strong, with such a big upper body – it can intimidate tigers in a conflict over an easy meal.

I agree with the concept, but wonder if maybe this isn't also a good argument for walking upright. People don't generally get attacked by tigers in Sumatra (they do in India, but there are many other factors there). Tigers seem not to think of people as a food source, so perhaps another animal that evolved to walk upright could benefit from this "other-ness" – the appearance of being outside of the normal food groups. Think like a tiger – you want the easiest meal, want to expend the least amount of energy to get it, and want to have the lowest risk of injury, as an injury can get infected fast in the jungle and kill you. Everything you eat has four legs and runs when it sees you. You spot something that doesn't have four legs, looks sort of big and strong, and doesn't run – in fact, it stares at you. Is it worth the risk? Nah, I saw a deer, a bunch of little pigs, and about a dozen rodents on the way here. What if a group of gibbons then evolved to be more grounded and became more nocturnal in the process – they would have different food sources than tree gibbons, along with different predators and different survival strategies, their physical traits would change with natural selection, and they would eventually speciate but retain some gibbon-like attributes – color, general shape, hairless face/hands/feet, etc. Even known gibbons run on the ground and are active at night occasionally. It isn't a great leap to imagine them exploiting a different niche and moving to a more terrestrial lifestyle.

Isn't OP just mistaken identity for a gibbon or an orangutan?

I would guess that some sightings are just that. People who aren't too familiar with local wildlife see a gibbon, an orangutan, or another known animal and jump to conclusions. Honestly, I thought this when I first got to Sumatra – OP was probably the rare, old, male orangutan that survived long enough to die of natural causes. Even people who see orangutans pretty regularly, rarely, if ever, see big, old males. Old orangutans actually get too large to climb trees and they look *freaky*! Their face plates and neck pouches grow to wild proportions, really distorting their appearance, their hair grows long and naturally dreads, especially the hair hanging off of their arms. They have been mistaken for wandering spirits, and I've read that the Dayak people in Borneo believe that all orangutans are ghosts of humans.

Getting up close with Pinkie and really listening to the descriptions of credible eyewitnesses made me realize the animal being described as an OP could not possibly be an orangutan. Orangutans' proportions and movements are completely wrong – they are much squatter, their legs are not long, their arms are disproportionately long, their torsos and legs would not be described as muscular, and when they do walk on two legs there is nothing comfortable or graceful about them. I tend to discount any reports of coloration because it is so varied in known species, but just the same, most reports of OP do not match the coloring of any known orangutan. Gibbons, on the other hand, are about the right height, certainly within the range of "could have been estimated incorrectly". They appear to have a broad, muscular upper body and shoulders, their coloration is correct, and they do walk with apparent ease on two legs. I've seen footage of them walking that I would even describe as graceful, almost dainty, like they're tiptoeing. I've never heard that particular phrase used to describe OP's gait, and would expect to if it was a mis-ID for a gibbon. I've shown people footage of gibbons walking and asked them to describe it – tiptoe, dancing, ballet-like, funny, cute, and other such adjectives were all used. Nobody said confident, strong, or impressive – all words used regularly to describe an OP's gait.

The pace and stride are also all wrong. Gibbons appear hurried when they walk, like their legs are a little too short to move the way they want to. They *almost* walk like a human, but not to the point where you could confuse them. I could see someone making a mistake, but really only at a distance – not up close, and not with an unobstructed view. Their arms practically touch the ground when they stand and something about them always looks hesitant, like a nervous child. OP is described by multiple witnesses as "confident", and that is not how I would describe a gibbon after being close to them and watching them in person.

The way OP is said to carry itself when walking seems distinctly "un-gibbon-like" as well. Almost all gibbons I observed walked with one hand raised above their head at all times, like they were volunteering to answer a question in class. OP is never described as adopting this posture. OP is, however, often described as "walking like a ghost", which predisposed me to the orangutan idea, but when I had this explained to me by Sahar and others, they said "with their arms in front of them, reaching for something". Neither orangutans nor gibbons really do this. They may reach for things to steady themselves or climb. In the case of gibbons, they can't get into a tall tree or structure fast enough – they'll even swing from a vertical sapling. They're just anxious to swing, and from anything, really. It seems that, if on the ground, they are only comfortable when using their long arms for something. OP is not – OP is described as walking, confidently, slowly, proudly, and upright.

Sahar's OP sighting where it grabbed the saplings may seem like a candidate for a gibbon swinging from a vertical source. I asked Sahar if it swung as it grabbed them the way a gibbon does. He replied that it did not – it grabbed the trees to move between them, the way a person would.

What makes me think it could be a hominin?
As usual, it really comes down to the penis. The descriptions of OP's genitals are not like that of any nonhuman primate. Among apes, only human males have "large" penises. The other apes' members are tiny – like, barely visible. Not only are they short, they are severely lacking in girth, even when erect. (Google it if you don't believe me, just not at work.) Apologies for all of the above to the male great apes out there, but it does explain their penchant for driving sports cars, as illustrated by the classic documentary *Lancelot Link, Secret Chimp.*

The description that Z and other eyewitnesses gave of a pendulous member is a feature as unique to humans amongst apes as walking upright. I would speculate that this particular attribute may actually be related to walking upright. In adopting an upright gait, humans experienced a change to their pelvic structure. This entire morphological shift is fascinating – the widening of the birth canal, changes to hip structure, etc. – but for our purposes here, the change also meant switching from mating "chimp-style" (from behind – why "chimp style" as opposed to "doggy style" hasn't caught on in the popular vernacular is beyond me) to "face-to-face" mating. Some theorize that this sparked a new intimacy and actually helped "humanize" us, giving us more of an emotional connection with our mates. It also appears to have driven the need for bigger penises, evolutionarily. If the theory is right, an upright-walking gibbon-like animal might mate face-to-face, and require a larger member.

Writing this reminds me of when I was four and, after watching a nature show on African mega-fauna, I casually asked my parents over dinner if people mated like hippos. My eight-year-old sister, who had a couple of her friends over, was mortified, but my father, without missing a beat, said, "Pretty much, but not usually in the water." He wasn't wrong. We humans have a lot of options for mating positions.

Penises aside, the fact that we know there were hominins very recently in Indonesia and do not know for a fact that a species of gibbon-like ground-dwelling ape ever existed means – of the two choices, the hominin is technically the most likely. But my gut tells me we are talking about two different animals whose stories have melded over the years, as mentioned at the start of this chapter. No matter what, I do believe this is worth further investigation, and fast. Jeremy and I talked about the possibility that OP, if it isn't already, could go extinct any day – there might be just a few individuals left, and, with over 17,000 islands to explore looking for remnant hobbits, researchers had better get out there. Jeremy has new camera-trap technology and a protocol that I think shows a lot of promise, but he needs funding. If I had the money, I would fund it. I believe he is the one person who really has a chance at finding this creature.

Unfortunately, both Mike Morwood and Sahar passed away not long after I met them. Mike from cancer and Sahar from acute kidney failure. Mike's contributions to the scientific community and our understanding of hominin evolution cannot be overstated. He was an amazing man, and I am privileged to have had the opportunity to speak with him. I was asked by famed cryptozoologist Loren Coleman to write a brief obituary for Sahar for the website Cryptomundo, and would like to end this book with it:

I'll remember Sahar as a kind, brave, and gentle man with an immense amount of respect for his forest. I was very sick while exploring Kerinci Seblat, and Sahar did what he could to help me. When we returned from a hellacious trip down the volcano, Sahar's wife prepared our entire crew one of the best meals I can remember, and they welcomed us with open arms into their home.

It was easy to dismiss some of the witnesses we came across on the series as attention seeking, exaggerating, or under-educated about local wildlife. Sahar was none of these. He was a humble man who genuinely wanted to know more about the creature he saw, which was different than any other animal he'd come across in his years spent in the forest. Anyone who spoke with him could not help but leave the encounter believing in the creature. This was a man at ease in the forest; understanding its mysteries and recognizing all of the subtle clues that gave away its inhabitants to his trained eyes. A sun bear has been here, there's a snake, check out this lizard… all invisible to me. Jeremy Holden and Sahar had a friendly competition to catch more species than each other… I was in way over my head when I joined in. When Sahar spoke of OP, he spoke of it with the type of longing that comes from someone who had experienced something remarkable, and wanted others to experience it as well.

It's a sad day for his family, his forest, and his friends.

Acknowledgements

While I dedicated this book to Nana, I truly could not have completed it without the help of the many incredible people I'm so fortunate to have in my life. I'd like to take a minute to thank each of them.

Anna – my phenomenal wife. She not only joins me on many adventures, but has put up with all of the insanity that comes with being a partner to a guy who does all of the stuff described in here.

Our kids, Luna Caulfield and Wallace Charles. The greatest aspect of my life is being a part of theirs.

My insane and wonderful family – Al, Mom, Sarah, and Nathan who have supported and encouraged me throughout my life. Mom, who learned more about alligator reproduction than she probably ever wanted to in her quest to support a budding young biologist and Al who took me camping and fishing despite having no interest in these activities himself, which I never knew until I was in my late twenties. Sorry about child welfare having to come to the house and watch you change diapers and question Sarah about possible neglect/abuse after I got salmonella from a lizard, then spread it to about a dozen friends, and cracked my head open sledding, and sliced my legs open sliding down a hill to catch a snake – hopefully this makes up for the embarrassment?

The entire current and past Icon family, particularly Harry and Laura Marshall. Harry and Laura are two of my favorite people on Earth. They are the people Anna and I want to be when we grow up. They are the smartest, nicest, funniest, and most caring and loving people you could hope to meet, and the greatest thing about doing TV has been having them enter our lives. We love them like family. In addition to Harry and Laura there's Andie Clare, Lucy Middleboe, Stephen McQuillan, Barny Revill, James Bickersteth, Alex Holden, Anna Gol, Ben Roy, Laura Coates, Sol Welch, Belinda Partridge, Abi Wrigley, Duncan Fairs, Robin Cox, Simon Reay, Brendan McGinty, and everyone else, who continue to be amazing forces of encouragement and support.

The Nat Geo team behind *Beast Hunter* – Janet Han Vissering, Steve Burns, Ashley Hoppin, Sydney Suissa, Russel Howard, Chris Albert, Geoff Daniels, Mike Mavretic, Dara Klatt, Steve Ashworth, Whit Higgins, and others. Thank you so much for your support and trust in allowing me to fulfill a lifelong dream, and letting Icon take the lead and make a series we are all really proud of.

The most amazing and supportive group of friends I could ask for – Adam Manning, Dom Pellegrino, Joe Viola, and Adrianna Wooden. Thank you for sticking by me and being there for me and my family through everything.

Thank you so much to the entire team at John Hunt Publishing, especially John Hunt, who saw the potential of the massive and messy manuscript I sent over, Dominic James, who assured all of my insecurities and answered all of my questions while reassuring me that it was all going to be okay, and the expert editing of Graham Clarke, who managed to pull these six books together and make them the cohesive series.

My very literary friends and family who served as the first reviewers of this book – Al Spain, Joe Viola, Dom Pellegrino, Richard Sugg, Sarah Franchi, Gene Campbell, Tim Fogarty, John Johnson, Zeb Schobernd, Sarahbeth Golden, and Luke Kirkland

– thank you for your insights and mocking. This book is much better because of you.

The folks at my day job who have supported my insane extracurricular activities – especially Bill O'Connor who gave me the opportunity to do this and assured me I'd still have a job when I returned.

Thanks to all of the incredible fixers, guides, and translators who kept us alive and safe, often risking your own lives in the process.

Thanks, finally, to the readers and fans of these shows! I hope you've enjoyed what you've seen and read! You can find all of my social media stuff at www.patspain.com. I try to answer questions and respond as best I can. Genuinely – thank you!

Continue the adventure with the Pat Spain On the Hunt Series

A Little Bigfoot: On the Hunt in Sumatra
Pat Spain lost a layer of skin, pulled leeches off his neither
regions and was violated by an Orangutan for this book
Paperback: 978-1-78904-605-2
ebook: 978-1-78904-606-9

200,000 Snakes: On the Hunt in Manitoba
Pat Spain got and lost his dream job, survived stage 3 cancer,
and laid down in a pit of 200,000 snakes for this book.
Paperback: 978-1-78904-648-9
ebook: 978-1-78904-649-6

A Living Dinosaur: On the Hunt in West Africa
Pat Spain was nearly thrown in a Cameroonian prison, learned
to use a long-drop toilet while a village of pygmy children
watched, and was deemed "too dirty to fly" for this book.
Paperback: 978-1-78904-656-4
ebook: 978-1-78904-657-1

A Bulletproof Ground Sloth: On the Hunt in Brazil
Pat Spain participated in the most extreme tribal ritual,
accidentally smuggled weapons, and almost lost his mind in the
Amazonian rainforest for this book.
Paperback: 978-1-78904-652-6
ebook: 978-1-78904-653-3

The Mongolian Death Worm: On the Hunt in the Gobi Desert
Pat Spain ingested toxic "foods", made a name for himself in
traditional Mongolian wrestling, and experienced the worst
bathroom on Earth for this book.
Paperback: 978-1-78904-650-2
ebook: 978-1-78904-651-9

Sea Serpents: On the Hunt in British Columbia
Pat Spain went to the bottom of the ocean, triggered a bunch of
very angry fisherman, and attempted to recreate an iconic scene
from Apocalypse Now for this book.

Paperback: 978-1-78904-654-0
ebook: 978-1-78904-655-7

Recent bestsellers from 6th Books are:

The Afterlife Unveiled
What the Dead Are Telling us About Their World!
Stafford Betty
What happens after we die? Spirits speaking through mediums
know, and they want us to know. This book unveils their world...
Paperback: 978-1-84694-496-3 ebook: 978-1-84694-926-5

Spirit Release
Sue Allen
A guide to psychic attack, curses, witchcraft, spirit attachment,
possession, soul retrieval, haunting, deliverance, exorcism and
more, as taught at the College of Psychic Studies.
Paperback: 978-1-84694-033-0 ebook: 978-1-84694-651-6

I'm Still With You
True Stories of Healing Grief Through Spirit Communication
Carole J. Obley
A series of after-death spirit communications which uplift, comfort
and heal, and show how love helps us grieve.
Paperback: 978-1-84694-107-8 ebook: 978-1-84694-639-4

Less Incomplete
A Guide to Experiencing the Human Condition Beyond the
Physical Body
Sandie Gustus
Based on 40 years of scientific research, this book is a dynamic
guide to understanding life beyond the physical body.
Paperback: 978-1-84694-351-5 ebook: 978-1-84694-892-3

Advanced Psychic Development
Becky Walsh
Learn how to practise as a professional, contemporary spiritual medium.
Paperback: 978-1-84694-062-0 ebook: 978-1-78099-941-8

Astral Projection Made Easy
and overcoming the fear of death
Stephanie June Sorrell
From the popular Made Easy series, *Astral Projection Made Easy* helps to eliminate the fear of death, through discussion of life beyond the physical body.
Paperback: 978-1-84694-611-0 ebook: 978-1-78099-225-9

The Miracle Workers Handbook
Seven Levels of Power and Manifestation of the Virgin Mary
Sherrie Dillard
Learn how to invoke the Virgin Mary's presence, communicate with her, receive her grace and miracles and become a miracle worker.
Paperback: 978-1-84694-920-3 ebook: 978-1-84694-921-0

Divine Guidance
The Answers You Need to Make Miracles
Stephanie J. King
Ask any question and the answer will be presented, like a direct line to higher realms… *Divine Guidance* helps you to regain control over your own journey through life.
Paperback: 978-1-78099-794-0 ebook: 978-1-78099-793-3

The End of Death
How Near-Death Experiences Prove the Afterlife
Admir Serrano
A compelling examination of the phenomena of Near-Death Experiences.
Paperback: 978-1-78279-233-8 ebook: 978-1-78279-232-1

Where After
Mariel Forde Clarke
A journey that will compel readers to view life after death in a completely different way.
Paperback: 978-1-78904-617-5 ebook: 978-1-78904-618-2

Harvest: The True Story of Alien Abduction
G L Davies
G. L. Davies's most terrifying investigation yet reveals one woman's terrifying ordeal of alien visitation, nightmarish visions and a prophecy of destruction on a scale never before seen in Pembrokeshire's peaceful history.
Paperback: 978-1-78904-385-3 ebook: 978-1-78904-386-0

The Scars of Eden
Paul Wallis
How do we distinguish between our ancestors' ideas of God and close encounters of an extra-terrestrial kind?
Paperback: 978-1-78904-852-0 ebook: 978-1-78904-853-7

Readers of ebooks can buy or view any of these bestsellers by clicking on the live link in the title. Most titles are published in paperback and as an ebook. Paperbacks are available in traditional bookshops. Both print and ebook formats are available online.

Find more titles and sign up to our readers' newsletter at http://www.johnhuntpublishing.com/mind-body-spirit.

Follow us on Facebook at https://www.facebook.com/OBooks and Twitter at https://twitter.com/obooks.